Theology
of the Body
for
Every Body

Leah Perrault

NOVALIS

© 2012 Novalis Publishing Inc.

Cover design: Blaine Herrmann
Layout: Audrey Wells

Published by Novalis

Publishing Office
10 Lower Spadina Avenue, Suite 400
Toronto, Ontario, Canada
M5V 2Z2

Head Office
4475 Frontenac Street
Montréal, Québec, Canada
H2H 2S2

www.novalis.ca

Cataloguing in Publication is available from Library and Archives Canada.

Printed in Canada.

We acknowledge the financial support of the Government of Canada through the Canada Book Fund for business development activities.

5 4 3 2 1   16 15 14 13 12

*For **Robyn** and **Eliot***

whose breath, bodies and lives
are a constant outpouring
of God's love, mercy and grace for me

and who graciously accept
my less-than-perfect gifts
with enthusiasm and wonder.

ACKNOWLEDGEMENTS

Anne Louise – Editing is an art and you are a master. This book is clearer, richer and more beautiful for the work of your hands. I am immensely grateful for your faith in me and for your generous sharing in the words of my heart and my life.

Grace, Joe and Novalis – This book was made possible because nearly a hundred young people crowded into the upper room of a Toronto pub for a presentation on *Theology of the Body*. It is a great privilege to have the trust of a Canadian Catholic publishing house. Thank you for your confidence – and your patience.

Brett & Flannery, Chris, Christy, Don, Jolyn, Kate, Kate & Chris, Kath, Keitha, Kieran, Lindsay, Lorell & Blake, Marie-Louise, Nancy, Ron, Teresita, Tony and Wade – Thank you for the conversations that fuel the fire I need to live faith and write about it. You call things out of me that I would not otherwise discover. There is no just return for what you have offered me – only the promise that I am looking forward to the next evening on the deck, talking and laughing over great food and a glass of wine.

Robyn & Eliot – Words fail to describe all the ways that you are amazing little people. Someday you will become aware that I have told so many of your stories before you had voices to tell them yourselves – so thank you for lending me your stories. I look forward to receiving your editing notes.

Marc – I appreciate all the Saturday mornings (and Tuesday evenings) you have spent playing dress-up and keeping kids away from the office door. So much of what you give to me is space and time to chase my strange and obscure love of things theological. Though you put up with my theological passion, you rarely acknowledge your own theological contributions: your eyes, your hands, your body are a revelation to me of God's love for me and for the world. In the few quiet moments of our lives at this stage, I am overwhelmed with wonder and gratitude that God has seen to it that we are living this life together.

CONTENTS

INTRODUCTION

Welcome to Being a Body

Perhaps the most profound gift I have received from Pope John Paul II is not his writing or his words. It was the gift of his presence in Canada at an important time in my life. When I left for World Youth Day in Toronto in 2002, I was fairly indifferent about the papacy. In my teenage years, I was blessed by very positive encounters with other Christian churches and traditions. I was skeptical, at the very least, about the significance of the pope, a single person, in the life of a church. I wasn't going to World Youth Day to see a pope, but to share faith with Catholic young people from all over the world.

But, as it happened, I was to arrive in Toronto late. The afternoon that John Paul landed at Pearson International Airport in Toronto, my group was already gathered at our host church. I was working at my summer job in Ottawa, in an office that constantly monitored TV news coverage. When I looked up from my computer, the image of the pope coming out of the airplane captured my attention. The sound was off, but I couldn't look away. An aging man, body bent and hands wrinkled, clinging carefully and with great attention to the handrail, walking intently down the stairs from his plane onto the tarmac. His body was filled with purpose and dignity, and I wanted to love him – not the pope so much as the man.

The next day, after a very late train ride and getting lost on the subway after midnight, I joined thousands of people at the exhibition grounds to officially welcome Pope John Paul II. Rather than vying for a spot right up front, I sat several hundred metres back under a tree, armed with my self-protection and skepticism. After I waited for hours in the heat and humidity, he arrived. What got me was not the crowd or the Popemobile, the words he would offer, or the liturgy. It was his eyes. They were a metre high on a Jumbotron. They pierced me, as if they were saying, "I love you. I love you like God loves you."

Then it was more than the eyes that spoke to me. It was his fragile, human body that communicated the deep and seeking love of a shepherd and the Shepherd. The wisdom and frailty of age, the effort of movement, the tears of joy. His body said what his words could not have convinced me to believe: God speaks our language, in flesh and blood, in eyes filled with tears and in damp, humid sweat – in the lives of popes and pilgrims alike.

Since my first encounter with John Paul, I have become more attentive to the ways in which our faith is nurtured by our experiences in the body. When was the last time you met someone without one – a body, that is? Our bodies are ever present but rarely at the front of our awareness, yet bodies are constantly bringing us the messages of other people, navigating our movement through the world, and communicating our thoughts, ideas and work without much direct attention. Only when we are ill or tired, or when we experience the uniqueness of our bodies, do we become more aware of just how much influence a body can have.

This book presupposes that we are called, as Christians, into the fullness of our discipleship at every stage of our lives, and that our bodies are essential to our spiritual lives.

Often it is the simplest of situations that call our attention to the blessings of being embodied. I love taking newborn babies to visit the elderly. In the midst of a nursing home, shrunken men, busy little ladies, those with ailing bodies and those living with Alzheimer's all stop what they are doing and turn their hearts to the smallest person in the room. They reach out beautifully weathered and wrinkled hands to touch perfect little fingers and toes. Their eyes are filled with wonder and purpose as they comb hair, adjust clothing and pour compliments on the baby's beauty. As the hardened bark of a mature tree gives way in the spring to tiny, fragile buds, the wisdom of age bears touching witness to the miracle of each and every new life.

The first kicks and movements of a baby in the womb are some of the most miraculous first signs of another person's presence in the world. We worship, as Catholic Christians, a God who became flesh, who kicked inside Mary's womb, who was born to a family who welcomed him. He healed the sick with the touch of his hand. He fed the hungry and gave water to those who thirsted. He understood the profound unity of our bodies and our souls, and he offered us salvation by his bodily death and resurrection. Jesus' body is essential to the action of God; as body of Christ, the church continues this mission in our bodies. When we burst, naked, into the world with vigorous cries or mere whimpers, we can almost hear the Spirit of God saying to us, as with Jesus, "Welcome to being a body."

PART I

Insight from Pope John Paul II's *Theology of the Body*

When I first heard about *Theology of the Body*, it was a trendy phrase used by eager Catholic university students to talk about the beauty of the church's teachings on sexuality. But most of the people I heard talking about it had never actually read it. When I cracked the cover, I discovered that *Theology of the Body* is a series of reflections that Pope John Paul II delivered at his Wednesday audiences in St. Peter's Square over about five years in the early 1980s. As I was born in the early 1980s, I didn't have the privilege of hearing them in person. I read them nearly twenty years later, and discovered a deep connection with a pope who took the body seriously.

Reading the pope's words as a university undergraduate and then rereading them as the major topic for my master's thesis, I became increasingly convinced that John Paul's words require either sustained, in-depth study or the assistance of interpreters for most people to access the wisdom of *Theology of the Body*. His language is academic and his style is more circular and mystical than linear or logic driven. He offers over 500 pages, collected in a series of reflections that were first offered to the church in the form of 133 weekly audiences, in a language that most of the original hearers didn't speak or understand.

In this work, the pope is speaking to people today. He acknowledges the fact that secular thinking has permeated people of faith. He is trying to bring an embodied perspective into a church that has suffered, at times, from sexual repression and disembodied spirituality, especially compared to cultures that are sexually obsessed and that disregard the reverence due the body. John Paul offers us creative ways to think about our humanity and God's plan for us. While it offers a contemporary reflection, *Theology of the Body* is at the same time grounded in the Catholic tradition, rooted in the Scriptures and deeply incarnational. It builds on the insights of other theologians, church documents and philosophers. It is not intended to be the only source of our theological reflection, nor does it encourage us to ignore or reject other important areas of spiritual thought or practice. Rather, John Paul offers us the gift of himself in this work. What makes it refreshing is that it is the work of a pope *and* a fellow human being who is striving to offer the gifts God has given him for the sake of the world.

Theology is the attempt to explain the mysteries of what we believe about God and about God in the world. In the case of *Theology of the Body*, John Paul turns to the mystery of the human body. Our bodies are essential to our humanity, to everything we do. Indeed, our entire spiritual lives are experienced in and through our bodies. If you have said a prayer lately, you have been attentive to positioning your body to focus on God. You have calmed your mind and your heart, formulated sentences in your brain and whispered them to God in the silence of God's love for you. If you have become aware of God's response to your prayers, you have felt comfort in the gentle easing of stress from your shoulders, the shivers of wonder and gratitude or the physical release of simply letting go of what was bothering you. Perhaps you have been disappointed that you felt nothing, expecting somehow that the desire of your heart would translate into some tangible, embodied sign that God hears you.

For nearly two thousand years, the Catholic church has insisted that humanity is defined by the joining of the body and the soul. Much of our spiritual thought, however, has focused on the movement of the soul through life and into eternal life. It is significant to John Paul that our spiritual life happens in the body – he reminds us that the road to God is this life, here and now. *Theology of the Body* has received a lot of attention in the area of married sexual ethics, and rightly so, but John Paul's writing is relevant for our whole lives, from birth to death, whether we are called to marriage, the single life, religious life or priesthood.

*

As the title of this book suggests, I believe that *Theology of the Body* has something to offer *every* person with a body. The first part, then, is an introduction to some of Pope John Paul II's foundational ideas about being a human person. It is not a summary of John Paul's text. The first part of this book introduces key ideas from *Theology of the Body* and attempts to reflect on the meaning of those key ideas when it comes to living out life in the human body. The second part of the book traces those key ideas through the stages and experiences of human life. My words are my response to John Paul's invitation to reflect deeply on the presence of God in every moment of our lives; I hope you experience this book as an invitation to do likewise. Such an exercise is not the only way to explore *Theology of the Body*, but it offers one way to see our own experience as part of the Christian tradition through John Paul's eyes.

Pope John Paul and his *Theology of the Body* have been great gifts to me, connecting what I have known deeply in my life in the body with the wisdom of the Christian tradition. I am not the only interpreter of this work, and I make no claims to have the only relevant perspective. If this book or others on this topic piques your curiosity, you may find yourself wanting direct, unfiltered and uninterpreted access to the words and ideas of *Theology of the Body*. I hope you will feel inspired to read John Paul's words for yourself.

CHAPTER 1

The Way We Think Changes the World

Whatever is true, whatever is honourable,
whatever is just, whatever is pure, whatever is pleasing,
whatever is commendable, if there is any excellence
and if there is anything worthy of praise,
think about these things.

~ Philippians 4:8

When Christopher Columbus set sail to find a passage from Europe to East Asia in 1492, he was convinced that there had to be a shorter route than the trip around Africa. His thought allowed him to set sail in the face of immense risk; the fact that he collided with what we now call North America dramatically changed the way Europeans thought about the earth's geography.

In the early 1980s, computers were the large and complicated experiments of a relative few. The first versions of the Internet attracted academics and highly skilled computer programmers and hobbyists, largely considered "geeks" by the rest of the world. Today, families scattered across the world keep in touch through video calls and Facebook. Businesses rely on email and social networks to keep in touch with employees and customers alike. We all look to tech experts for help with our gadgets. When we go to write something and reach for our computer instead of a pen, we reveal the extent to which technology has worked its way into our thoughts and our actions.

In 1970, when Sasha was eleven, she sat down at her desk at school only to discover that it had been vandalized overnight. The words were quickly washed off, the offender was punished, and the teacher and her friends assured her that the message was a lie. But over the forty years since that day, the message remains tattooed inside her eyelids: "Sasha is ugly, and no one wants to look at her." Without consciously knowing it, she has believed in the truth of that message so completely that she has shut out friends who complimented her, turned down jobs where she would have to be a visible face for the company, and tried to earn God's love instead of accepting it freely. Her thoughts have changed the way she has interacted with the world.

What would happen if all the people on earth, all of God's people, really understood the truth about our humanity? What would happen if we loved ourselves and each other as much and as well as God loves us?

Before we can understand *Theology of the Body*, we need to know that John Paul was a philosopher before he was a theologian, a playwright before he was a priest. He was inspired to write because he experienced the "incessant confrontation of doctrine with life."[1] For John Paul, philosophy is not a dirty word, an academic field devoid of practical reality. The ideas and beliefs of faith were constantly lived out and made real in his everyday life. He wrote plays about faith and love, books about the consequences of human action, encyclicals about human work. His writings make it clear that he wrote because he believed that changing our thoughts could change the world. *Theology of the Body* is a collection of his thoughts about humanity, offered so that we might become more fully human by putting those thoughts into practice.

Faith lives in the space between our thoughts and our actions. Here our beliefs and our lives intersect: we live out our faith with our whole selves: our conviction and emotion, our breath and being, our spirits and bodies. When we take on Christianity, we *become* Christians. The vision of Jesus becomes our vision; his life becomes our life. The truth of faith is not something we own, to be put on a shelf and framed, or preserved in a jar for display in a museum. Faith is thought set on fire as it permeates

1   Pope John Paul II / Karol Wojtyla, *Love and Responsibility,* 2nd ed., translated by H.T. Willetts (San Francisco: Ignatius Press, 1992), 15.

the body. Christian faith is alive and breathing, oozing with the Spirit of God, aching to change the world.

As Christians, we are motivated to visit the sick and the imprisoned, feed the hungry and clothe the naked because we think that Jesus was right to do so, and because we believe he has called us to follow him. Contemporary self-help books constantly remind us that attitude shapes ability. When the disciples were worried that it was too hard for people to get to heaven, Jesus reminded them that "for God all things are possible" (Matthew 19:26). Philippians 4:8 reminds us that if we seek justice, purity and truth, we need to allow our actions to be fed by our thoughts. Our world is indeed a different place when we adjust the way we think.

In the space between infancy and about age five, children go through a phase in their development where there is no boundary between reality and imagination. Nightmares are especially scary because these beautiful little people have no conceptual framework to differentiate the monster in their mind from the real and safe and loving arms of their parents. Hannah is three. When she wakes up screaming in the night, her mom rushes in and soothes her, saying, "You're okay. It was just a dream. I'm here." The next day, when asked what she was dreaming about, Hannah has forgotten, but she says, "I was dreaming about God." Her mom asks what God was like, and Hannah responds immediately: "Like a rainbow."

Somewhere along the way, as we become adults, most of us learn to define the boundaries between reality and imagination so rigidly that we find it hard to let our imaginations affect reality. Forgetting that God is a mystery, we define God so clearly in our minds that we do not recognize him in rainbows. We get settled into thinking about God and ourselves in the same ways we always have. If we want to see the world as God sees it, we need to expand our thinking about God.

You are reading this book because you share a conviction that ideas matter, that thoughts are powerful, that God acts through our changes of heart. You read because you believe that the things you think can take shape in your life and in your body. I hope this book contains a thought or two that will affect your world. But those thoughts will not be only my thoughts. They are my thoughts about John Paul's thoughts, colliding with your thoughts. Together, we can think about what it means to be human and to live out that humanity in our bodies in a way that makes this world a more loving place for people to discover God.

QUESTIONS FOR REFLECTION

1. I worry more than I should, and I am addicted to doing. For many years, I have kept a little card inside a drawer in my desk, taped to the corner of my computer screen or stuck on my fridge. It says, "Be still and know that I am God. ~ Psalm 46:10" What quotation, song lyric or idea has shaped the way you try to live? What difference does that idea make in your life?

2. Think of a person (friend, teacher, author, etc.) whose thoughts always give you a new and exciting perspective. Who are the people whose thoughts change your world? What is your relationship with those people? How do you feel when their ideas collide with yours?

3. "Conversion" is the religious word for a dramatic change of heart and direction. When have you changed your mind about something big, turned around and taken steps in a new direction, had an experience of conversion? How did your thinking change over days, months or years to facilitate that change?

CHAPTER 2

Experience Matters

"Who do you say that I am?"

~ Mark 8:29

During Jesus' ministry, his disciples experienced life with him. In the Gospel of Mark, they watch Jesus feed the hungry and heal the sick. He tries to teach the disciples, but at times, they don't see what Jesus is trying to show them, and neither do the religious leaders of the day. When he retreats with his disciples, Jesus asks them, "Who do people say that I am?" The disciples tell him that some people think he is John the Baptist, or Elijah, or a prophet. He then asks them, "But who do you say that I am?" Jesus knows they do not understand everything he is trying to teach them. In the midst of their confusion, they search their experience of Jesus for the answer. And Peter answers, "You are the messiah." Those closest to Jesus, those who have known him and have experienced him, are able to put their faith in him.

God knows that our knowledge begins with our experience, and chooses to meet us there. God reveals himself to us in our humanity, most obviously by becoming one of us in Jesus. Born in a stable, refugee in Egypt, lost in Jerusalem, tradesman in Nazareth, itinerant preacher, innocent prisoner. This Jesus knew the smell of a barn, the love of his parents, the demands of working, the pang of hunger, the pain of torture and the solitude of death. Jesus discovered his divinity and his humanity by living out his life. We worship a God who knows the experience of being human.

When Pope John Paul reads about the creation of the world in Genesis, he insists that God's revelation is related to human experience. The pope writes that our humanity "is perceived by us above all in experience."[2] This idea is at the heart of an embodied spirituality. To be human is to live in the mystery of the body: to see, hear, smell, taste and touch the world around us. Everything is mediated by the body. We think with our brains, love with our hands, pray on our knees.

Jesus reaches across history, calling out for people to follow him, asking each of us, "Who do you say that I am?" In *Theology of the Body*, John Paul suggests that if humans are to know anything about ourselves and God, we begin with our experience. He says that "*our experience is in some way a legitimate means for theological interpretation*" (TOB 4:4). He is not suggesting that our personal experiences are the only source of revelation about God and God's people, but he does acknowledge that our stories are important; they are foundational to how we understand ourselves and God.

I have found that it is impossible to have a notion of either myself or God that does not draw in some way on my experience. At the same time, I have found that my own experience is not always as reliable as I would like to think it is. If you've ever sat down to dinner with a large group after listening to a political debate, going to a concert or seeing a play, you know that every person in the room experiences the same events differently. Our personal experiences are *subjective*. We interpret them in different ways at different points in our lives. New experiences give us a fresh perspective on the old ones. A huge part of living and learning is a growing appreciation for the gift and limits of human experience – both our own and that of others.

> When John Paul uses the words "subjective" and "objective," he is not using them the way most of us do. In its modern, scientific use, "objective" usually refers to something that can be proven and is free of bias. Subjective, then, is the opposite of objective –

---

2   Pope John Paul II / Karol Wojtyla. *Man and Woman He Created Them: A Theology of the Body*, translated by Michael Waldstein (Boston: Pauline Books & Media), 4:4. All subsequent references to this work will be cited in the text as TOB.

it cannot be proved and is inherently biased. We can be tempted to live our spirituality with a worldly "objectivity," rigidly adhering to a prescribed set of rules that we perceive to be the guarantee of our salvation; conversely, we can be tempted to avoid all communal conflict in spirituality, falling into a "subjective" relativism that makes each person the master of his or her own truth.

John Paul's use of these terms cuts through the polarity created by the way we typically use them. "Objective," in *Theology of the Body*, refers to that which is relevant to the whole. "Subjective" refers to that which is particular within the whole. For the pope, the subjective and the objective are not opposites, but rather, they are two dimensions of the same reality.

Truth always has an objective and a subjective dimension. For example, persons share an objective humanity, but no one person experiences the world in a way that represents every human person that has ever been and will be. Gravity is an objective reality, but we do not experience the whole weight and consequence of gravity holding the solar system in place – we only feel the force against our own bodies when we jump and are pushed back to the ground, and some of us jump higher than others.

Objectively, we can say that God loves humanity. But we say that because many unique people have experienced God's love through creation, through their friends and family, through the particular circumstances of their lives, and have shared those subjective experiences with others. It is the collective conviction of a large group of people over a long period of time that convinces us that the statement bears an objective truth, because it has emerged in a diversity of ways, at a subjective level.

Daniel was raised Catholic. He was baptized within a week of being born. His family went to Mass every week and prayed the rosary for peace every evening. He spent two mandatory weeks in catechism classes every year, right in the middle of summer holidays. When the other kids were playing outside and having fun, he was stuck with forty other "prisoners" in the sweltering heat of the small-town church basement, reciting lines from the Baltimore Catechism. Jesus was the man on the crucifix on the wall, the reason Dan was sweating bullets and not throwing baseballs.

He memorized a sentence about God loving him, but he never really thought about it much. He stopped going to church altogether when he left home, but when he got married, he and his wife moved back to his hometown, and going to church was something that good families did. Now that he is in his fifties, when Daniel listens to the readings at Mass, Jesus seems to be more like a good parent than a dictatorial fun-wrecker. In fact, the only way he can imagine God's love for him is to think about how he feels when he looks at his kids, and at their kids.

In her early twenties, Aimée comes from an agnostic family and has two good friends, Shen and Kesia, who are Christians. Her understanding of Jesus has pretty much been limited to her discussions with them and a few services over the years. Her friend Shen might actually be Jesus, as far as she can tell. Shen goes to church regularly. He gets frustrated with the people in his church sometimes, but he works hard to love them. He hangs out with teens at an inner-city youth shelter on his days off, and when he talks, it feels like he's preaching – the good kind of preaching that makes her want to believe in God. Kesia is really vocal about faith having a place in public debate. She goes to church when it doesn't conflict with something else, and she talks a lot about Jesus as a political activist. Aimée isn't sure which friend has a more accurate understanding of Jesus, though some days she thinks she'd like to find out.

Eric grew up aspiring to be a priest. As a small child, his parents often found him "playing church" with his sister. He wanted to help people, to pray with people who were sick and dying, to baptize babies, and to get invited over for dinner with all the families in the parish. When he was seven a new priest moved to town. Over two years, the priest gained Eric's trust and took advantage of him. When Eric's parents found out what had happened, they stopped going to church and got their son an excellent therapist. Thirty years later, he is a well-adjusted, healthy man. He talks openly about the abuse and the process of recovery in his work as a crisis counsellor. But when he talks with his closest friend about faith, Eric says he feels empty and betrayed. He used to love Jesus, and he thought he knew a Jesus who loved him. But he feels disconnected from God and doesn't know if anything can be done about it.

Daniel, Aimée and Eric each have unique and real experiences of God. When we put them all together, however, we can be tempted to talk about whose experience is "right." If we give in to that temptation, we are forgetting that it was Jesus who asked the question "Who do *you* say that I am?" God created each of us. He shares our experiences with us. He desires that we will come to know him ourselves, in the particular experiences of our lives. John Paul insists that our experience matters because it is the only way we can come to know God. But if my experience matters, then so does yours – and so does everyone else's. My experience and understanding of God will be enriched by listening to and loving Daniel, Aimée and Eric, by sharing life experience with them.

Limited though our experience may be, the moments, places and feelings that make up our lives are all we have. When we share our experiences with others, developing relationships of love and trust, we start to care about what they have experienced. We listen more closely, receive advice willingly, ask more questions. Theology is the discipline of faithful people seeking a deeper understanding of God. A theology of the body seeks to know the mystery of God in our bodies, in the sights and sounds that invite us to see and hear what God loves about the world. As we discover God in our experiences, it is only natural that we turn Jesus' question back to him: "Who do *You* say that I am?" When we ask that question, we join the many other human beings before us who have turned to God to make sense of their experience.

QUESTIONS FOR REFLECTION

1. What are the three most significant experiences of your life? Why have they had such a profound effect on the rest of your life? Have you always known they were significant, or did their importance become more apparent over time?

2. Do you trust your own experiences? Is it difficult for you to name when and where you have experienced God? Why or why not?

3. What experiences have shaped your understanding of who God is? Are your experiences similar to those of other people you know? What do the differences between your experiences and theirs teach you?

CHAPTER 3

The Bible as Experience

But Moses said to God, "Who am I that I should go to Pharaoh, and bring the Israelites out of Egypt?"

~ *Exodus 3:11*

Sometimes when we listen to the readings at Mass or pick up a Bible, we distance ourselves from the people we read about. It is easy to do, really, since I have never heard the voice of God speaking from a burning bush, for example. Moses responds with a familiar dose of self-doubt at God's call: you must have the wrong person. He sees himself as a simple shepherd, not so well spoken, and definitely powerless to free a people from slavery. But God knows who Moses is. This story is Moses' story – his experience of God. And it is God's story – God's relationship with his people.

The Bible is a collection of stories. Many Christians, especially in the Catholic church, feel a bit ill-equipped to understand the stories in the Bible. But stories are important. Stories shape the way we think, the way we approach problems, the way we make meaning of our lives. When children are first exposed to books, they develop attachments to their favourite stories. They listen as if they don't know the ending, memorize the words and ask for the same book over and over again. When we are facing difficult decisions, we often relate to characters in novels more easily than we can interpret rulebooks. Jesus knew this. He taught with parables because stories speak to us in powerful ways.

Stories emerge in all kinds of forms: songs, poetry, novels, comic books, history texts, fables, fairy tales, novels, biographies, movies, TV shows, and the list goes on. Some stories are true and others are fiction, but even artistic pieces have the capacity to speak truth, even though they do not recount actual events. A Catholic understanding of the Bible requires us to appreciate that it is a collection of books and stories of many genres. Some of the Bible contains history of specific times and places, like the books of Kings and Judges. The Psalms and the Song of Songs are poetry and music. The story of Jonah is a fable, a warning that those who don't listen to God should beware the belly of the big fish. The gospels are a sort of historical biography, each written for a different early church community at a different time. Romans and Corinthians are letters to the Christian communities at Rome and Corinth.

This collection of stories that we call the Bible speaks to the truth of God. The stories are told by people much like us. They are the stories of people of faith and doubt, real-life people, people seeking and searching to know God.

The authors knew they were writing something meaningful, important, even sacred. But they did not write their stories knowing that these would become our Scriptures. The books of the Bible were written by human hands, infused with the Spirit dwelling inside them, overseen by a God who knew what these accounts would one day become. Over the fourth century, the early church leaders gathered at church councils to review the many words that had been written during the history of the Hebrew people and in the first centuries of Christianity. The books that now make up the Bible were selected from a range of texts on the basis of their theology and their use in prayer and liturgy by early Christian communities. The bishops of the early church, gathered at a church council, agreed on the books and stories that would become the most foundational and authoritative stories for our lives.

The Bible is the Word of God, spoken to us through human words and experiences. The Word of God is so real and powerful that it is actually another person – the person of Jesus. The mystery at the heart of our Christian faith is that our God becomes human: "And the Word became flesh and lived among us" (John 1:14a). When we read the stories of the Scriptures, we reach out to touch the Word of God. We encounter the person of God (Father, Son and Holy Spirit) through the words and experiences of people who have sought God throughout history.

John Paul relies on Scripture in every chapter of *Theology of the Body*. He looks to a biblical experience and then asks what it can teach us about our experience. He starts with the creation stories in the first few chapters of Genesis. When he talks about experiences of the first persons, he calls them the "original experiences." He invites us to go to the beginning of creation with him, to listen to the story with new ears, and to find new meaning in a very old experience of being human.

And so, with John Paul, let's start at the *beginning...*

QUESTIONS FOR REFLECTION

1. What Bible stories or characters are your favourites? What do you love about them? How are they real for you?

2. What stories, characters or passages of the Bible leave you feeling confused or disconnected? What do you do when you feel this way?

3. If someone were to read your journal, poetry, ancestral lineage, family history, novels or recipe books in a few hundred years, what would they learn about you? What would they learn about the God you worship?

CHAPTER 4

Taking the "Beginning" Seriously

God saw everything that he had made, and indeed, it was very good.

~ Genesis 1:31

Pope John Paul begins *Theology of the Body* with Matthew 19. The Pharisees are talking about divorce and asking Jesus why he says that divorce is not okay when Moses gave the Israelites exceptions to the rule. Jesus responds by quoting Genesis 2:24: "Have you not heard that for this reason a man shall leave his father and mother and be joined to his wife, and the two shall become one flesh?" Jesus explains that it was hardness of heart that resulted in the exceptions, but "from the beginning it was not so" (Matthew 19:8b). This quotation sends John Paul back to Genesis, to discover what Jesus wants us to know about the "beginning."

In the opening pages of the Bible, there are two creation stories. The first creation account is Genesis 1:1 to 2:4. John Paul calls this account *objective*, in that it tells the story of the creation of humanity, but does not talk about the unique persons. God is the primary character in the story, and the world takes shape as a response to God's Word. The text is beautiful and theological.

The second creation account is Genesis 2:5 to 3:24. Though it follows the first account in the Bible, this version of the story is the older one. It depicts God as a character much like the first persons. Adam and Eve interact with God in the garden, naming the animals and influencing the action of the story. John Paul calls this text *subjective*, because it depicts people as unique subjects, giving us a window into their personal experience of God and creation. It is this account that Jesus quotes when he suggests that the beginning matters.

John Paul spends most of the first chapter of *Theology of the Body* on the second account of creation, because it offers us a window into subjective human experience. He calls our attention to four *original experiences* of the first persons: solitude, unity, nakedness and shame. He identifies the experience and then explains what we learn about humanity from the experiences of Adam and Eve.

Original Solitude. In the second creation narrative, God creates one person significantly before the second one. This time of being alone before God is what John Paul calls original solitude. During this time, God recognizes the need for the person to have a partner, and so creates the animals and the birds. The person gives them names, but no suitable partner is found. The first person learns about being a person, alone before God, but also in relationship with God. The person is discovering the beauty and fullness of creation while longing to have someone to share it with. Original solitude teaches us about our subjectivity: the way our experience of God in the world is unique from everyone else's. And the yearning of the first person tells us that our solitude is not the fullness of our human experience.[3] Part of the experience of solitude is the longing for unity.

Original Unity. When God creates the second person, the first person wakes and exclaims, "This at last is bone of my bones and flesh of my flesh" (Genesis 2:23). After experiencing solitude, the yearning for community is realized in the presence of another human being, separate and the same. While they are not the same person, they share humanity, relationship and the love of God. Unity makes sense only with reference to solitude. John Paul proposes that these experiences are a pair; both indicate a truth of our humanity on their own, but each is fully true only with reference to the other. It is in the absence of another that we

---

3   John Paul notes the contributions of biblical scholars who remind us that in the original Hebrew, the first person is not referred to as male until after the creation of the female. This is important for John Paul because solitude is a foundational experience of all humans, not just of men. In fact, John Paul insists in *Theology of the Body* that both male and female are created in the image and likeness of God, that male and female are two ways of being human. See *Theology of the Body*, 8:1, 9:1-5.

learn that we need each other. For John Paul, the experiences of solitude and unity allow the first persons to discover the giftedness of creation: that we are created *for* – for one another, for relationships of love, for communion. To be human is to participate in the giftedness of creation. We receive the gift of life, the gifts of creation, the gifts of other people, and we become gifts to one another. To be human is to be loved for our subjectivity and to have a place in an objective human family.

Original Nakedness. This experience is just one line from Genesis: "And the man and his wife were both naked, and were not ashamed" (Genesis 2:25). For John Paul, physical nakedness is a sign of being completely open and without fear before another being. Not only are the man and woman naked, but they don't know that there is any other way to be. They exist in a simplicity of knowing the deep and intimate reality of one another without effort. This nakedness is not merely physical nakedness. The nakedness of the body corresponds with the nakedness of the spirit and the absence of fear and shame. When we are physically naked, we are exposed and vulnerable and we feel emotionally and spiritually laid bare as well. This is why nakedness is reserved for the most intimate, trusting and loving relationships in our lives, where our physical, emotional and spiritual well-being are sustained. Like solitude and unity, the meaning of the experience of nakedness is deepened with the introduction of shame.

Original Shame. When Adam and Eve choose to eat of the tree of the knowledge of good and evil despite God's instructions, their eyes are opened and they immediately cover themselves. In addition to making clothing, when God comes to the garden, they hide. Adam and Eve know they have disobeyed God. Their sin is carried out and felt in their bodies, reflecting the state of their souls, and they express their shame by covering their bodies and hiding. John Paul suggests that the experience of shame introduces fear. Having failed to live up to God's call, we become fearful of the gift – of ourselves and others. We start to worry that we will fail, that others will fail us, that we are not worthy of giving or receiving the gifts God has for us. Shame is the opposite of nakedness, where Adam and Eve are able to be in relationship with one another without fear of rejection, deceit or devaluing.

Every time I reread *Theology of the Body*, I am inspired by the way John Paul makes the story of the "beginning" so real. His telling of the story makes me imagine I have met Adam and Eve. Though the story is the subjective, personal experience of these first persons, John Paul invites us to share our subjectivity with them. And when we look at other people, hear their stories and connect them to our own, we begin to touch on what is shared between us. We move from the solitude of our own experience to the unity of our humanity. The "beginning" is not just the "beginning" of the first persons. The "original experiences" are the stories of the Christian community, of all human beings. They are our experiences, too.

QUESTIONS FOR REFLECTION

1. When you think about God as the Creator, what stands out for you in creation? Why?

2. What do you like about each of the two creation stories in the opening chapters of Genesis? What is unsettling about each of them?

3. How do you feel about "beginnings"?
   What beginnings in your life continue to be significant? Why?

CHAPTER 5

The God Story
Continues in Our Stories

"Where you go, I will go; where you lodge, I will lodge;
your people shall be my people, and your God my God."
~ Ruth 1:16

When John Paul asks what it means to be a body, he returns to our theological beginning, to creation, to the stories that have given meaning to the people of God since the beginning. He calls these creation stories our "theological prehistory" (TOB 4:1-3), because they are the shared experience of the human family. The Bible is the experience of God's people, and in that sense it is also our experience.

I have always loved to read, and engaging with the experiences and thoughts of people in books has always come naturally to me. When it began to happen with Scripture, though, I was hesitant to tell anyone about it. I didn't want to sound weird. But more than that, I didn't want to have the stories taken away from me, to be told that I was wrong, that God's story couldn't be my story.

When I was twelve, my grandfather became very ill. My dad came home from a family meeting with the doctors and told us that they thought we had about ten days to say goodbye. I was devastated. I remember curling up on the wide windowsill after I was supposed to be in bed. I opened the blinds and stared up at the stars, bright and clear from the relative darkness of the farmhouse. I begged and pleaded with

God: "You raised Lazarus from the dead. You can save Grandpa. I'm not finished with him yet." I felt, like Mary and Martha, that God had waited too long to act, had let things go beyond repair. As it turned out, Grandpa lived another sixteen years. From the impossible, life grew up out of the ashes. I have no way of knowing if my prayers affected his healing, but the experience was a miracle of biblical proportions for me.

I kept finding that the stories of the Scriptures were being retold in my life, and I saw it happening in other people, too. John Paul's *Theology of the Body*, when I finally read it, gave me a language to explain what was going on. Our experiences are scattered and subjective, constantly shifting in meaning as we have new experiences and gain fresh perspective. I kept finding meaning for my experiences when they came into conversation with the experiences of the people in the Bible stories. When I read the stories of the people in the Bible, I wanted to cry out with Ruth, "Your people shall be my people and your God my God." And so it is with the "beginning." The original experiences are my experiences, our experiences. They touch what it means to be human.

When we live out the truth of our humanity, entering into our lives with purpose and seeking God in our conversations, our families, our work, our rest and our play, we become aware of the God story playing out in our stories. As Christians we are called to read our own stories alongside the scriptural stories, so that our lives become a witness to the grace of God, not unlike the Gospels themselves. In reading *Theology of the Body*, the connections begin with the original experiences.

Solitude. In original solitude, the first person noticed the beauty of creation and then noticed there was no one to share it with. We do not learn about solitude by reading Genesis for the first time. We experience it long before we have language to describe it. Babies cry when they discover that they are alone. Toddlers follow their parents into each and every room in the house. Gradually, a child learns that he can be alone and still be safe. An adolescent starts to enjoy the time she spends reading or listening to music alone in her room. We feel our solitude when we are chosen last for a sports team, when we find the courage to go to Mass on our own in a new city, when we are ready to be home after a long business trip, when we sit for weeks on end in a seniors' residence, hospital or prison without a visitor.

Solitude is both a gift and a challenge of our existence. We are essentially separate beings, unique in creation and before God. Despite this separateness, we are persons created for relationship, with God and with other people. Solitude is experienced in many ways, but is perhaps most profoundly felt in our longing (to be touched, understood, at home) and our suffering (especially when others cannot ease it). The body itself is a sign of this solitude. Our skin clearly marks the boundaries of our bodies. The circulatory and nervous systems are closed, providing nourishment and information for just one body, except during pregnancy, when solitude coexists with unity in the same body. Solitude is a miracle that draws us out of ourselves and into each other.

Unity. Solitude and unity are paired experiences. The original experience of unity is the deep recognition of shared humanity with another person. Solitude is not eliminated by the experience of unity – each of us continues to exist as a unique person created and called by God – but unity gives purpose to our solitude. We are created *for* relationships, and we are moved beyond ourselves by the joy we find in each other. The first persons are created as adults, speaking and walking, finding love and commitment as first expressions of their being. John Paul suggests that our creation as male and female is a sign of our creation *for* unity, but sex is not the only experience of unity.

When we forge a deep friendship, fall in love, offer forgiveness, we say with Adam and Eve, "This at last is bone of my bone and flesh of my flesh." We experience unity when someone reaches quickly for our hand when we are about to fall, when we feel truly listened to and understood, when we find a community that feels like home. We experience unity when we marry and when we hold our children. And we feel our creation for unity deeply when we sit with someone who is dying. The experience of unity is sometimes a deeply private encounter, such as when spouses make love, or when a nurse cares for a patient in the middle of the night, but the experience of unity has an expansive dimension that should make us more capable of seeing and caring for the image of God in every person and in all of God's creation.

Nakedness. Original nakedness is the experience of being laid bare without fear. We experience nakedness when we approach one another for forgiveness and seek reconciliation. It is nakedness that surrounds us when we finally hit rock bottom and seek out help for an addiction. We experience nakedness when we put ourselves out there, take a risk and share a radical idea in a classroom or a workplace. We are naked when we stop giving each other the silent treatment and respectfully ask for what we need. We experience nakedness in accepting our weaknesses and refusing to believe that they make us unlovable.

Nakedness is a physical, spiritual, emotional, intellectual and social reality. When we are tiny, we rely on our parents for every kind of care, including diaper changes, feeding and transportation. We are naturally naked without shame. As we grow, we come to know the difference between nakedness and being clothed. We learn that we can be honest or dishonest. We can share what we are thinking or be afraid that our thoughts will be rejected or mocked. Our feelings emerge; we can develop a sense of comfort and the ability to manage our feelings appropriately or not at all. We can offer ourselves to our families and communities generously or we can hoard our gifts for ourselves. The kind of nakedness that John Paul is talking about is a freedom to offer our whole selves in honesty to others for our mutual benefit according to God's call, without fear or shame.

Nakedness is naturally associated with sexuality, given that the outward sign of our sexuality is embodied in our male or female bodies. Our bodies, in our male or female form, proclaim our creation for relationship with the other. Every relationship of our lives has a sexual dimension, because we are created male and female. Sexuality is the fire in us that draws us out of ourselves, makes us wonder at the beauty of creation, keeps us in awe of miracles, and makes us delight in the mystery of others. Sexuality allows us to create, to spend our energy, to sacrifice, to love. Original nakedness affirms the gift of our sexuality, without being exclusively focused on our sexual activity.

Shame. Our experience of nakedness is affected by the experience of shame. When Adam and Eve eat of the tree of the knowledge of good and evil, they immediately cover themselves. They become fearful of the truth of their humanity, worried that they are bound by solitude, incapable of unity and in danger when they are naked. Shame is the rejection of the trust of nakedness, a long look in the mirror where I begin to believe the nasty things that others have said about my hips, my hair or my ears. It is the experience of believing that I am only as good as the sum of my weakest parts, which I must spend my lifetime trying to hide from those I hope will love me.

Most of us are more than familiar with the experience of shame. We steal dignity from others, obsess about what we do not have, or run from the truth. We find ourselves lying, saying something hurtful or avoiding someone to protect some vulnerable place in ourselves that we are only rarely willing to acknowledge. We judge people and are terrified of their judgment. We pretend to be the people that we think others want us to be instead of believing in the goodness of our true selves. We belittle, cheat and abuse, and then we justify our actions. When we cannot justify, we hide, burying our brokenness in the darkest place we can find.

When I sit down to prepare for the sacrament of Reconciliation, I usually begin by calling to mind "the things I have done and the things I have failed to do." But these things are not in and of themselves the fullness of my confession. Underneath my speaking harshly, begrudging, judgment and pride is my fear. I criticize because I am afraid that recognizing the strengths and gifts of others will render me less needed. I refuse to forgive because if I let go of my need to be right, I might be left wrong, in need of forgiveness that someone else will refuse in the same way I do. I make judgments out of fear that God's judgment won't come quickly enough, in the way I think it ought to, or will be more merciful than fair. I need to believe I have earned the gifts and blessings in my life to prevent the kind of generosity that would extend them to others, out of fear that God's abundance is limited. Shame is the way the conscience acknowledges the illegitimacy of our fears, even while we hold fast to our sinfulness as though it can protect us from vulnerability. Somewhat ironically, the sacrament of Reconciliation offers us a way through shame via the beginning: we come alone and lay ourselves bare before God, in the presence of another, a sign of our belonging to the community. We choose a naked vulnerability to the truth of who we are, broken and blessed.

This story is our story. Solitude, unity, nakedness and shame are foundational because we experience them over and over again in different ways, reinforcing basic truths about our human experience. But neither our stories nor the God story begin or end with shame. Christian life begins by joining our story to the God story and entering into the mess of being God's broken body. In *Theology of the Body*, John Paul insists that we are called beyond the experience of shame to live out the truth of our humanity in the body, to become the people we were created to be from the "beginning" (TOB 46:6).

QUESTIONS FOR REFLECTION

1. When have you experienced solitude, unity, nakedness and shame? How has God been present in those experiences?

2. When has your own experience given you confidence? When have you found comfort and consolation in the experiences of others?

3. How is the God story continuing in your story? Have you ever felt like Dinah (Genesis 34), Jacob (Genesis 33:22-32), Hannah (1 Samuel 1-2:10), David (1 Samuel 17), Job (Job 40:3-5), Martha (Luke 10:38-42) or Judas (Mark 14:10-11)?

CHAPTER 6

The *Spousal* Meaning of the Body

*This is the body: a witness to creation as a fundamental gift,
and therefore a witness to Love as the source from which this same
self-giving springs.*

~ *Pope John Paul II, TOB 14:4*

So often in my life, I find myself totally captivated by the beauty of a single person. Most recently it happened with Suzanne. I met her when we were having coffee with a mutual friend and I just can't get enough of her. She's this deep listener with a fierce sense of purpose. She asks amazing questions and she is inspired, rather than threatened, by the gifts of others. She has a small frame and a funky sense of style – her body seems to breathe fresh air into the world around her. She is a sign to me of the way that God loves. I can't help falling in love with her over and over again. And she's not the only one ... which leaves me thrilled at the idea of how fabulous God is.

The body is not just a vehicle to transport our souls from birth to death: our bodies are the expression of our souls, the external manifestation of the Mystery that dwells in each of us. Have you ever had a moment where time seems to stand still and you see the body of someone you love in a new way? The eyes seem like glass, reflecting all the beauty of the person. Instead of hands, you see the weathering of years of service in wrinkles, tendons, calluses and scratched knuckles. In the profile of a child, you see four generations across two families. This is the mystery of the body: that it holds the mystery of God's creation, seen and unseen.

Pope John Paul returns to the beginning because he believes that Jesus points us there for a reason. Original solitude, unity and nakedness teach us that all of creation is a gift from God. We ourselves are signs of the abundance of God's generosity, overflowing with the capacity to love, to create, to give. John Paul suggests that human consciousness of the gift of creation is what makes us unique from the rest of creation. We can "respond to the Creator with the language of this understanding" (TOB 13:4). When we discover that our existence is a gift, the only fitting response is to give ourselves back to God. This is the *spousal* meaning of the body.

Throughout the Scriptures, marriage is used as a metaphor for God's relationship with God's people, because the lifelong commitment and love of spouses is one of the most powerful human experiences of God's faithfulness. Before Jesus arrived in history and we received the presence of God in the sacraments of the church, we had a sign of God's faithfulness in the love between husbands and wives.[4] John Paul does not refer to the meaning of the body as *spousal* because marriage is the best or universal vocation, but because the mutual self-giving of spouses is a sign of the kind of self-giving that humans have been created for at every stage of our lives – free, generous, selfless, abundant and deep.

As Christians, we follow Jesus, who offered the most full and abundant spousal gift in human history – on the cross. Whether we are three days old or nearly ninety, whether we are married or single, a doctor or a religious sister, the meaning of the body is spousal.[5]

---

4   Pope John Paul calls marriage the "primordial sacrament" because he sees the first human sign of God's covenantal love in the experience of Adam and Eve. From the "beginning," before the Word of God became flesh, John Paul argues, marriage has been part of God's plan for salvation, a sign of our creation for relationships and a practical way in which we participate in God's refining us for communion with him. See *Theology of the Body*, 96–99.

5   The third chapter of *Theology of the Body* is a long explanation of the way in which celibate vocations fulfill the same spousal meaning of the body. (See *Theology of the Body*, 64–83.) This makes even more sense when we consider that we all begin life unmarried. The meaning of the body is spousal from the moment we are conceived, in relationship with another, preparing to offer ourselves to the world with every act of love.

We are called to make gifts of ourselves that will change us and change the world. The Bible reminds us that Jesus,

> though he was in the form of God,
> did not regard equality with God
> as something to be exploited,
> but emptied himself,
> taking the form of a slave,
> being born in human likeness.
> And being found in human form,
> he humbled himself
> and became obedient to the point of death –
> even death on a cross. (Philippians 2:6-8)

Jesus empties himself. To the point of death on the cross. And his emptying brings about new life – for him and for us. Jesus shows us that God's loving is an active pouring out of himself – full, generous, selfless, abundant and deep. We are created in God's image to be poured out for ourselves and for others. This idea demonstrates the essential unity of our bodies and souls. The spiritual meaning and purpose of our lives cannot be pursued apart from or independent of the body. Whether we follow Jesus or deny him, we do so in the body, and our actions always have spiritual consequences.

Self-giving to the point of self-emptying is a radically countercultural idea. We can be tempted to hold onto ourselves, to love as though we have been given a limited quantity, as though we might waste it and be left loveless if we give too generously. But love is not a finite resource. In fact, the more we offer, the more we have. And just as Jesus shows his love for God by pouring himself out for us, we love God by loving each other and the world.

When Pedro was diagnosed with a terminal illness, he was angry. He had spent his whole life working towards retirement and now, with just two months of work remaining, he was sitting down with his wife to plan his own funeral. Filled with bitterness and resentment, he cried out to Nalini, "I've wasted my life banking on a future I won't get to have! And I've taught our kids to do the same." She held him as he sobbed. "It's not too late," she whispered. Pedro decided he would not be angry anymore. His wife was right. He quit working immediately and arranged to use some of the money he would have used for golfing in retirement to bring his three children, their families and a few family friends to their home-turned-hospice for a week. Pedro and Nalini planned Christmas in September, celebrating all the family rituals and traditions that would be dramatically changed in just four months' time. Pedro died two weeks later. His kids had a new take on the meaning of their lives and their work. It was not the way he had hoped to teach his children about life's blessings, but it worked, perhaps even better than the retirement he had planned.

Our experience matters because it is in the everyday acts of love that we participate in God transforming us into God's holy people. In order to discover the *spousal* meaning of our bodies, our humanity, we must be willing to let go of everything, to fall in love with everyone. Our lives are a long lesson in learning to let go into God and into each other. We can pour ourselves out with freedom when we recognize that our lives were never ours in the first place – they have always been a gift from God.

QUESTIONS FOR REFLECTION

1. Life's experiences are felt in both our souls and our bodies. Falling off a bicycle. Laughing until you cry. Being thrown into a lake. Running a marathon. Accomplishing a goal. Being too sick to breathe. Giving birth. Giving something away that you desperately want for yourself. Riding a zip-line. Cleaning up a mess you did not make. When have you experienced yourself being poured out in and through your body?

2. What other words could be used in place of *spousal* to describe the meaning of the body? What word resonates most deeply with your experience of the self-giving purpose of human life?

3. What feels unfinished or difficult in your experience of giving yourself for the sake of others? What do you cling to? What do you find easy to let go of?

CHAPTER 7

The Body as Sacrament

"Lord, when was it that we saw you hungry and gave you food, or thirsty and gave you something to drink? And when was it that we saw you a stranger and welcomed you, or naked and gave you clothing? And when was it that we saw you sick or in prison and visited you?" ... "Truly I tell you, just as you did it to one of the least of these who are members of my family, you did it to me."

~ Matthew 25:38-40

Sometimes when I invite people to connect their story to the God story, to find God in the moments of their lives, someone reacts with anger and fear. "How dare we be so presumptuous? We are sinful and broken." It's true. We are sinful and broken, but we are also the body of Christ in the world, and we will not experience new life if we hide in the upper room. If fear is a consequence of original shame, we are called to find a way through it.

John Paul insists that the spousal meaning of the body remains even after the experience of sin. The body is not irreparably damaged by sin. *Theology of the Body* rests on the *sacramentality* of the human body. The body "enters in to the definition of the sacrament, which is 'a visible sign of an invisible reality'" (TOB 87:5). This foundational idea of the Catholic faith insists that our spirituality requires *stuff*.

In oceans and sunlight, turning leaves and fire, we see something of the invisible mystery of God. We worship in holy places, baptize with water, light the Easter fire. The feast of the Eucharist makes sense because we have been fed around kitchen tables, nourished by the food and the care of our families and friends. We follow a God whose body was nailed to a cross. John Paul puts it this way: "The body, in fact, and only the body, is capable of making visible what is invisible: the spiritual and the divine. It has been created to transfer into the visible reality of the world the mystery hidden from eternity in God and thus to be a sign of it" (TOB 19:4). The self-giving of God is visible in the very *stuff* of creation, most notably in us.

The sacramentality of the body is the "scandal" of the Incarnation. In Christianity, the language of the sacred becomes a word, *a Word made flesh.* Our God takes on our humanity and sanctifies it. Jesus was born into all the earthiness of human existence. He was formed in the womb, cell by cell. He kicked at the flesh of Mary and most assuredly heard the voice of Joseph through her belly. He was born in a barn, laid in straw. He cried, learned to walk and talk, fell down, scraped his knees, got mud in his hair, came in for supper with dirty clothes. He wondered in adolescence about who he was, and had to discover his own vocation and mission. His humanity was as real as ours. Despite his refusal to sin, he faced the same temptation, fear, despair and confusion that life offers to us all.

John Paul reminds us that a sacrament is not just something holy, to be put on display. A sacrament is "a sign of grace, and it is an efficacious sign. It does not merely *indicate* and express grace in a visible way, in the manner of a sign, but *produces* grace and contributes efficaciously to cause that grace to become part of [humanity] and to *realize and fulfill the work of salvation* in [us], the work determined ahead of time by God from eternity and fully revealed in Christ" (TOB 87:5). Our bodies are essential to the way in which God loves us and loves the world. They not only witness to the divinity of God and the dignity of people, they bring grace into the world and participate in the ongoing work of God's creation.

When we are scandalized by the humanity of Jesus and by the sacredness of our own lives, we are living out of the precise fear that was initiated in the experience of original shame. In *A Return to Love,* Marianne Williamson touches the heart of our fear at the holiness of our humanity:

Our deepest fear is not that we are inadequate. Our deepest fear is that we are powerful beyond measure. It is our light, not our darkness that most frightens us. We ask ourselves, Who am I to be brilliant, gorgeous, talented, fabulous? Actually, who are you *not* to be? You are a child of God. Your playing small does not serve the world. There's nothing enlightened about shrinking so that other people won't feel insecure around you. We are all meant to shine, as children do. We were born to make manifest the glory of God that is within us. It's not just in some of us; it's in everyone. And as we let our own light shine, we unconsciously give other people permission to do the same. As we're liberated from our own fear, our presence automatically liberates others.[6]

Our humanity is holy. We are God's vessels for love in the world. We are called, alongside Mary and John the Baptist, to let our lives point to Jesus, to allow God to be present to us in the mess, even when we would rather he just took the mess away. When Jesus commissioned his disciples, he asked them to bring the good news to the world, to continue his mission of serving those most in need. When we care for the sick, clothe the naked, feed the hungry, share the good news, we not only care for God's people, we are Jesus and we care for Jesus.

We can be easily incapacitated by our fear that such a calling is beyond us. The calling is certainly beyond me – alleviated somewhat by the growing awareness that God's plan is bigger than me – but it also includes me, for better or for worse. And even though I can't wrap my brain around this plan, I will place my hope in God, who orchestrated it this way for a reason.

---

6   Marianne Williamson, *A Return to Love* (New York: Harper Collins, 1996), 190–91.

QUESTIONS FOR REFLECTION

1. Who has been a sacrament of God in your life? Who has spoken words that seemed to come from God? Who has been God's hands holding you up? Who radiates God's love in your world?

2. Let one of your fingers release its grip on any fear you have of being a sacrament, a visible sign of the awesomeness of God. When have you been an "efficacious" sign of God's love for the world?

3. Think of a particularly wonderful celebration of one of the sacraments (Baptism, Confirmation, Eucharist, Reconciliation, Anointing of the Sick, Marriage, or Ordination). What everyday experiences were connected to that celebration? How was the body (or bodies) engaged in that celebration?

4. How might the idea that your body is *sacramental* change the way you live?

CHAPTER 8

Hope: A Christian Way
of Seeing

"Do not be afraid!"

~ *Pope John Paul II*

In Chapter 1, I said that Pope John Paul II was a philosopher before he was a theologian, a playwright before he was a priest. When a photographer captures a scene from a rooftop, we can see things that we do not see from our place on the ground. When a historian uses a different philosophical approach to writing history, we can see that there is more than one side to a story. Faith should also offer us new perspective. Like art and philosophy, faith can be a different set of lenses with which we see the world.

John Paul wrote *Theology of the Body* to affect the way we see the body and its essential role in our spiritual life. While the experiences of solitude, unity and nakedness create a picture of our innocence and a vision of what we have been created for, original shame has been used too often to keep us from believing that God is still calling us. We live in a broken world, with too much suffering. Many philosophers in our day are suspicious about everything, especially faith. But John Paul calls us back to the beginning with the knowledge of the end of the story: Jesus rises from the dead and leaves the tomb. Christians are called to be people of hope.

John Paul is not suggesting that we ignore our sinfulness or that we could go back to a time before shame. He is proposing, by his insistence that the beginning matters, that we seek an ever-deepening appreciation of what it has always meant to be human. We are to follow Jesus with hope that we have inherited a love that is deeper, more freeing and more powerful than our darkness and fear. Christian hope is not merely secular optimism, a sort of perennial "glass is half-full" attitude that keeps us smiling even when it rains the entire weekend of the outdoor family reunion. Christian hope is deeper. It is our sustenance when our children are suffering, when we battle mental illness and when our doubts in God seem larger than our faith. The world has enough injustice and evil to obliterate optimism when violence destroys families and recruits child soldiers, when people die of starvation and curable diseases and when abuse plagues the bedrooms and kitchens of our families and neighbours. Our God goes into the tomb and comes out alive.

Sr. Evelyn hadn't wanted to go to Brazil in the first place. Her order sent her there just three weeks before Christmas and she cried herself to sleep every night for the first week. And then something miraculous happened. Gabriella ran into Sr. Evelyn on the road the next day and invited her for lunch. Three little boys played on the floor at Gabriella's feet while she prepared the meal. Observing how little this family had and feeling embarrassed, Sr. Evelyn, in broken Portuguese, offered to help. Gabriella smiled and told her to sit. "I heard you crying last night," she said with a smile. "I think you need a mom to make you lunch." When Sr. Evelyn returned home after four years in one of the poorest communities in Brazil, her family thought she would be home for good. She got off the plane, walked into the airport, and greeted them with big hugs and a huge smile. She let her sister take her bag and picked up her nephew in her arms, while she looked her parents in the eyes, saying, "I need you to know that this is just a visit home. I'm going back to Brazil in two weeks." Sr. Evelyn knew it would be difficult for her family to hear she was going back. But she wasn't going because the Brazilian poor needed her. She was going back because she needed them. In the midst of poverty, she had found a people who knew what it was to have hope that Jesus could lift them off the cross.

If the body is to be a sacrament, a place where grace can ease our suffering, then we need to hold fast to hope. John Paul says that the human person, after the experience of shame, is always called and never condemned. If we are going to find ourselves in heaven one day, then we must constantly experience God calling us to be fully human. John Paul says that "redemption is a truth, a reality" to which we are "called, and called with effectiveness" (TOB 46:4). Though we are tempted by all kinds of sin, the beginning is a reminder that we were created for more. Jesus sends us to the beginning because our creation in God's image is powerful, and because his suffering, death and resurrection have made it possible for us to have hope that we are not essentially condemned to sin.

Alexei is a guard in a prison. He's been working there for fifteen years. Every day when he goes in to work, he hears extraordinary stories of sin, shame and brokenness. He holds the keys that keep these people locked up. More often than not, he leaves the prison feeling overwhelmed and powerless to help the men and women he encounters. But, each morning, when he walks to the prison, he prays the Prayer of St. Francis. He repeats one line to himself between visits when things are especially difficult: "Where there is despair, O Lord, let me sow hope." Alexei doesn't know it yet, but next week, nearly a hundred former inmates are planning an event at the prison to thank him for his work. Some of them have stayed out of jail, some are still battling addictions, and others are back in jail for another round, but they all want Alexei to know that the way he cares for them is not typical. He gives them hope. He believes in them when they give him every reason not to, when they have stopped believing in themselves.

The experience of shame introduces us to fear – fear that we are not good enough, fear that God cannot love us, fear that we will never be more than the sum of our sinfulness. In *Theology of the Body*, John Paul says to us again, Do not be afraid. He invites us to have hope in the God who believes in us, who hopes in us. He invites us to hope in each other, to see what God sees. In God's eyes, even though we might mess it up, we are "always essentially 'called' and not merely 'accused'" (TOB 107:6).

When I was studying theology, as I was sitting in class one day I became overwhelmed by a sort of hopelessness at the thought of the brokenness of the world and the church. It was just before Easter and I got a bit lost in my thoughts. I was thinking about the disciples after the crucifixion, about how so many of them scattered and abandoned Jesus. I was thinking about the few who stayed. A few of the people who had given up their lives to follow Jesus went and asked for his body. Though he had tried to tell them what would happen, they hadn't understood. Confused, in the midst of their grief, these few people did the only thing they knew how to do. They lovingly prepared Jesus' body for burial. They removed the nails, anointed his body with oil, wrapped him in a clean cloth. Without the knowledge we have of his rising from the dead, they simply cared for the broken body of Christ. My thoughts returned to the class and I was filled with a new hope. I am called; we are called: "called with energy," in the midst of our brokenness, to care for the broken body of Jesus.

We have to stop worrying that sin is lurking around every corner, just waiting to destroy us. Even while we resist the temptation to sin, we must start believing that we cannot run from the love of God, that love will hold us no matter where we go, that God will provide the patience and strength, wisdom and faith, courage and hope we need to be the Body of Christ and to care for the Body of Christ on earth. When we change our perspective about who we are, where we come from and how God sees us, we can see with the eyes of hope. And beyond merely seeing with the eyes of hope, John Paul offers us a way to live it out as he calls us from our experience into embodied action that will change us and change the world.

QUESTIONS FOR REFLECTION

1. Have you ever written a word so many times that it doesn't look like the same word anymore? Take several minutes to look in the mirror. Look at yourself long enough that you start to look unfamiliar. Look at yourself and imagine how others might see you. Reconnect with the self that *you* see in the mirror. How do you think God sees you? How would you see yourself with hope?

2. What are you afraid of? What experiences led you to be afraid? What would have to be different for you to let go of that fear?

3. What gives you hope? How do you stay connected to God's hope when you are faced with difficulty, suffering or fear?

CHAPTER 9

Being and Becoming Human

"If any want to become my followers, let them deny themselves and take up their cross and follow me.
For those who want to save their life will lose it, and those who lose their life for my sake, and for the sake of the gospel, will save it."

~ *Mark 8:34-35*

So it turns out that *Theology of the Body* is actually a book about how we live our spirituality in and through our bodies. Interestingly enough, Jesus did not say that those who want to be his disciples should read his book and then use it to tell other people that they are wrong. Christianity is not primarily an intellectual endeavour. Though thoughts can change the world, faith is ultimately about how we are pursued, loved and transformed by the Word of God and about how our actions change the world in light of God's first loving us.

Jesus invites us to *do* something, to "take up their cross and follow him." The very thing we are called to do is to offer the gift of ourselves, as Jesus does. When John Paul suggests that the meaning of the body is spousal, he is saying that we were created to lose our lives for Jesus, so we can find the life we were created for.

Some people have wonderful, dramatic stories about the moment or moments they decided to lose their lives for Jesus' sake. My story is not the story of a dramatic single moment of change. Over the course of my entire life, I have been offered the chance to choose, again and again, to take up the cross and follow Jesus. Sometimes, more often than I would like, I choose wrong. And every time, God offers me the choice again.

Most of the people I meet who have an interest in *Theology of the Body* have not read it, but they have the impression that it is a book about ethics, a sort of rulebook about sex. John Paul does have something to say about sex (which you can read more about in Chapter 13), but as you may have noticed, it is my conviction that his book is mostly about what it means to be human. The misconception that *Theology of the Body* is primarily about ethics arises at least in part because John Paul believes that who we are and who we become is shaped by how we act.

That was an important line. If you remember only one thing from this book, it should be that line: *who we are and who we become is shaped by how we act*. Most of us know this by experience. Jill is a bully. She uses her body to intimidate people, yelling at them when she is just inches away from them. When verbal assault fails her, she has been known to resort to her fists. Everything in her life seems to have fallen apart when she realizes that she has violently pushed away everyone who used to care about her. She wants to change, and she knows that if she wants to have friendships and relationships again, she will have to start behaving differently. She will have to behave herself into a different way of being Jill.

Over the course of *Theology of the Body*, John Paul begins with experience and arrives at action.[7] He says that we begin with experience, form understanding, develop values and act out of that experience. Think about the original experiences. We *experience* being alone and together, being naked and ashamed. We come to *understand*, with John Paul, that we are unique in God's image and created for community. Our nakedness is the truth of who we are, and shame makes us doubt that we are worthy. If we follow Jesus back to the beginning, we learn to *value* our solitude, unity and nakedness, even while we refuse to be mastered by shame. Only then can we *act* according to our dignity, in a way that allows our bodies to be effective signs of grace. This seems to be a linear

---

7 In *Theology of the Body*, John Paul starts with the "beginning" and ends up with a reflection on the action of natural family planning. It takes over 500 pages to get there. This paragraph, chapter and book are very simplified versions of John Paul's ideas. If you want to read more about the journey from experience to action, see *Theology of the Body*, 79:9, where John Paul describes, relatively succinctly, how the experience of celibacy is an expression of the spousal meaning of the body. The longer philosophical foundation can be found in his book *The Acting Person*, especially in chapter seven.

process, but we go through this process over and over again as we have new experiences, gain new understanding and adjust our values before acting again.

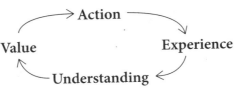

John Paul suggests that this process is how we, as human persons, are the authors of authentically human action. Our action is directed outward at the world, affecting other persons and things. But our action is also directed inward, affecting us.[8] Take Jill, for example. She was not born a bully, but she experienced from an early age that she could get her way by throwing fits and hitting. Since her behaviour was not challenged, she came to understand that it was effective. She valued getting her own way and being in control. After a time, she even came to value intimidating others, inspiring fear in people. And so she acted in ways that gave her control, scared people, made her feel powerful by making others powerless. It was the experience of isolation, loneliness and destruction of relationships that one day woke her up to the idea that perhaps she was misunderstanding reality, that she had placed value on things that were not ultimately making her happy.

Jill's aggressive and violent behaviour made others scared. They pushed her away, creating a safe distance for themselves. When people did get close, Jill's interaction almost always brought out the worst in people – yelling, passive-aggressive communication, insults or lies. The environment in Jill's world was always tense and explosive. These were the outward consequences of her actions. Inwardly, Jill was also changed by her behaviour. Every time she screamed at someone, she became a little less capable of believing in her own goodness. Hitting people made her scared of being hit. When she finally broke down and started to reach out for help, she discovered that the person she had destroyed the most was herself.

This is why actions matter. When we act in holy ways, we participate in the work of God, redeeming, refining and beautifying the world. At

---

8   Pope John Paul II / Karol Wojtyla, *The Acting Person*, translated by Anna-Teresa Tymieniecka (Boston: D. Reidel Publishing Co., 1979), 351.

the same time, our holy actions participate in God's refining us – we participate in our own salvation. When we sin, we work against God, damaging others, creation, our relationship with God and even ourselves. We distance ourselves from God, eating away at our own willingness to receive God's grace and help.

When we have a disagreement with someone, it is usually over a visible action. The diagram above has action on the top because, in my experience, this process of human understanding and action is mostly like an iceberg, with only the external actions of the body being visible to those outside the individual person. When Jill pushed her colleagues around, no one could see the experience of her childhood, where she got away with everything and had no boundaries placed on her by loving parents. No one else could see her misunderstanding of power. Her deformed values were visible only in the way that she physically and emotionally disregarded the needs of others.

When Jill's eyes were opened and she saw what she had been doing to others and to herself, someone's words finally connected her action to her experience. She had just finished yelling at a brand-new employee, and instead of slinking away or reacting loudly, as others had done, Mason calmly took a step back from her body and said, "I don't know who hurt you. I cannot know how you have experienced the world. But I will not treat you like you have just treated me. This is your one free opportunity to yell at me. If it happens again, I will not be coming back to work."

Jill left work for the day as soon as Mason left her office. As she walked home, she passed the church her parents occasionally took her to as a child. For some reason, she stepped inside. She sat in the pew and looked up at the man on the cross. She saw Mason, and everyone else she had been beating down with her words and her body and her anger, in Jesus. And she saw herself. She was broken and destroyed. She was too tired to go on living this way. Maybe this God could be her God. Maybe this God could love her this broken.

This is why it is so important that the God story becomes our story. When our experience gets connected to the experience of God and God's people, we start to have a new understanding. Our values shift and begin to reflect God more clearly. Our action will change only when we have changed our values and have reinterpreted our experience to form a clearer understanding.

Who we are and who we become are shaped by how we act. Ethics are rules that foster healthy and holy relationships with ourselves, each other and God. The *objective* call that God offers to each and every one of us is holiness – holiness that will fulfill us, refine us and make the world more beautiful, loving and compassionate. As persons, each of us experiences that call *subjectively*, in the particular circumstances of our lives. Every moment of every day, we will be called to pour ourselves out, to give ourselves to God and to each other in a way that will change the world. We will be called by Jesus – alongside the first disciples – to lose our lives so we can find them. We will be and become human by the way we behave in grocery store checkouts and while driving our cars. This is John Paul's gift in *Theology of the Body*. It will take us a lifetime to live it out.

QUESTIONS FOR REFLECTION

1. Why do you choose to follow Jesus? How does the way you live your life reflect your experience of Jesus?

2. When have you made a judgment about someone else's actions, only to discover later that you had misjudged them? Did the discovery give you an insight into the experience, understanding and values of another person?

3. Over the course of your life, when has your story been most clearly connected to the God story? When has it been disconnected? How do your experiences, understandings, values and actions play out in these two realities?

4. What ethical convictions do you hold most closely? (Some people feel morally obligated to recycle and others cannot tolerate dishonesty.) How do your experiences, understandings, values and actions contribute to and reinforce your convictions? How has God's story shaped those convictions?

PART 2

Living the Theology
of Our Bodies

When I dream about heaven, I think about sitting down with God and talking until the early hours of the morning. I want to have one of those long conversations where we know we will have a lifetime to talk but it still doesn't seem like enough time to really hear everything we want to hear and to say all that needs to be said.

I want to know how God dreamed up the beauty and mystery of life. I want to know why he created mosquitoes and what he was thinking as he formed the mountains. The size and colour of the prairie sky seem to be a window into the magnitude of God; and I want to fly with him and in him. When I hear the sound of snow crunching under my feet and feel my cheeks and thighs tingling with cold, I want to breathe the visible breath of God, steaming from his mouth. I want to dive into God, and feel the relief I feel when a cool lake embraces my sunburnt limbs and satisfies my thirsty soul.

I want to know how Jesus anticipated his own humanity, how it felt to breathe the first time, and the depth of his grief when Joseph died. I want to hear the Son of God talk about creation and history and suffering. I want to know what the events of my life have been like for Jesus, in the moments when he reached out and touched me, carried me and rejoiced with me.

I want to dance with the Holy Spirit, to have some concrete understanding of that which is not embodied. I want to feel the connection of my spirit and God's Spirit. The language of the Spirit fills my broken words and my speechlessness – I need to learn that language of silence and the groaning of the soul. I want to delight in the purity of the Spirit with my whole body. I want to know and touch and feel the delight of God.

I want to see the world the way God sees the world. Every so often, I am startled from my daydreaming to realize that this conversation has already started – here and now – in the moments that make up my life.

The rest of this book is not about how John Paul presents his ideas but about how we live out his ideas in our bodies. The rest of this book is about how his ideas have taken flesh in my life and in the lives I have been privileged to witness and to share. The names and details of these stories have been changed to respect the privacy and dignity of the people who have so generously shared life with me.

This book is a starting place, an invitation to see our lives as the sacred ground of redemption, the place where God is seeking us and longing to love us. As you read, I hope you will find yourself distracted by your own stories of grace, and that the God story will emerge ever more clearly as you recall the details of your own life.

CHAPTER 10

Come and Follow Me

But we have this treasure in clay jars, so that it may be made clear that this extraordinary power belongs to God and does not come from us.

~ 2 Corinthians 4:7

When Jesus showed up on the shore where Simon and Andrew were fishing, I doubt they anticipated what was coming. If they had, they might have called in sick that day, out of nervous anxiety. When Jesus asks them to follow him, the Bible says, "Immediately they left their nets and followed him" (Matthew 4:20). Simon and Andrew meet Jesus and they are changed. The experience of hearing God's call gives them a new understanding of the purpose of their lives, the meaning of their bodies. Their values shift and they are able to let go of the lives they had before and follow him. One day, when they were fishing, they connected their stories to the God story.

Their response seems dramatic – as yours might seem. But their lives had been filled with experiences, understandings, values and actions that made it possible for them to say yes to Jesus in that moment on the beach. I was born into a Catholic family and baptized when I was a few months old. The call of Jesus has been a part of my life since before I have memory. When people ask me when I had my "conversion," I usually look a bit stunned and say something like "Every day." I remember putting on my favourite frilly dress to go to church as a very small child. I remember making a choice in a playground game to include someone whom it

54

would have been easier to exclude. Faith has long been the desire of my heart and an intentional choice in my life. Every morning, God offers me another day to follow him: by getting dressed, eating breakfast, going to work, taking care of my kids, loving my husband and taking soup to the neighbours who just had a baby. Twenty years ago, my response looked different – I went to elementary school, put on puppet shows, had sleep-overs, set the table and loaded the dishwasher. Following Jesus today looks different than it did when I was a child, and will look different again in thirty years, but God's call remains in the routine moments of each day.

Theology of the Body assumes that God is calling us, that God desires every person to come and follow him. Some of us are more comfortable than others thinking of ourselves as disciples. In a world that is critical of religion, it can be intimidating to claim faith as our own. But Jesus doesn't offer us private or partial memberships. Following Jesus requires our whole lives. Still, being a disciple does not mean becoming discon-nected from reality. In fact, discipleship is about connecting ourselves with the deepest truth of reality, who is God.

When we choose to follow Jesus, we say yes to God's universal and *objectively* human call: to become fully human, in this life and for eter-nity. God's plan for our lives, however, is particular and *subjective*. Each of us will live out our discipleship on the unique roads of our own lives. Being a disciple is as simple – and difficult – as showing up for the mo-ments of our lives.

Pope John Paul II says that the meaning of our bodies is *spousal*. This body is a mystery, a sign of God's divinity in the world, and for that reason we need a lifetime to figure it out. But, at a practical level, John Paul is asking us to be attentive – to who we are and who God is. Living *Theology of the Body* means paying attention to our lives because they are holy and because they are the places where we ourselves will become holy.

Janelle grew up in a family that attended church services a couple of times a year. When she went to a Christian summer camp the year she turned fourteen, she discovered that faith was about Jesus and not about sitting still and quiet for an hour. When she got home, she decided she could walk to church by herself.

Carlos has gone to church his whole life. Lately, he has been feel-ing guilty because he seems to have more doubt than certainty when it comes to God. Sixty years of Sundays is an awful waste of time if he's been wrong all this time. With the same sort of urgency he felt when he proposed to his wife, he's been feeling a deep need to ask all the questions he has ignored for years. He feels like a hypocrite, exploring his doubt after raising his kids to go to church. But, if there is a God, surely God can handle a few questions?

Sr. Daria was finally ready to move and open the hospice that had been her dream since she joined her community. She had arrived home with the last load of moving boxes when the phone rang. Her sister's voice was full of panic: "Dad. He's had a stroke." When everything was settled, Sr. Daria was moving home instead of to the hospice. Her life was taking a turn she hadn't expected, and the hospice was going to have to wait a little longer.

When Janelle met Jesus at summer camp, she had no idea that some-day he would ask her to care for a son with autism. Carlos' wife did not join her husband's church knowing that one day she would be asked to walk with him while he asked unsettling questions. Sr. Daria knew that God had a place for her to care for the sick and the dying, but she had never imagined she would be caring for her own dad.

When we agree to follow Jesus, we don't get a blueprint outlining the rest of our lives. God calls us in the present moment and we agree to follow one step at a time. Discernment is the big word for our decision-making process as we consider God's invitation. Sometimes the decision is immediate, obvious, easy. Other times, the decisions are bigger, harder, less clear. Discipleship is about continuing to say yes, as openly as we can, even while we struggle with that decision.

Discernment is the art of paying attention to God, in all the places God might show up. For most of us, God's call is not an audible voice, a mystical vision or flashing road signs. Most often, God's voice emerges in our distractions. Someone asks for change on a street corner. A young couple is digging a car out of the ditch without success. An elderly person sits down on a bench beside us and starts chatting. What's more, God calls us *not* to act as often as he calls us to do something. A colleague tosses us an insult and is waiting for a comeback. A friend is battling addiction and is looking for someone to enable him. Children are trying to work out an argument. Sometimes we are supposed to keep quiet, to let go, to resist interfering, to stop giving long enough to receive. Gentleness, waiting and receptivity are as faith-filled as boldness, activity and selflessness. When we follow Jesus, we discern how we offer ourselves as gifts in the experiences that make up today.

When we think about Jesus saying, "Come, follow me," we may get hung up on figuring out our "vocation." We spend a great deal of our early lives worrying whether we are called to marriage, single life, religious life or priesthood. And then we worry that we chose wrong or that others have it easier. Pursuing God's plan this way seemed inevitable until I found myself crying with my spiritual director one day. I was married, with a baby, working in ministry and having some hard days. I was worried that I had taken a wrong turn and that God had not called me to this painful place. The priest smiled and said, "God has been calling you your whole life, and he certainly isn't going to stop now. He cannot call you anywhere but where you are." The conversation was one of the most inspiring of my life. I often recall it with a big grin, a reminder that God is calling me here and now – and that gives me great joy, almost all the time.

God does not have a plan for your life that you have to decode carefully in order to avoid going off course. God calls you wherever you are, no matter how bad it has become, to be a gift to yourself, to others and to God. We do that by taking our experience seriously, listening to and learning from the experiences of others, learning the God story, paying attention to the wisdom of the church, taking time to pray, and, in the end, making the best decisions we can with the information available to us. We will certainly make mistakes, but we can be assured that when we continue to listen for God, we will not find ourselves in a place where God has stopped asking us to come and follow him.

Most of the time, following Jesus seems pretty ordinary. But every so often, we have a glimpse of what God is doing in us, through us and around us. After Gilles spent months working on tedious paperwork and endured six more months of silent waiting, a family of refugees will be able to stay in Canada. Stacey has been at home with kids for fifteen years, changing diapers, making meals, mediating arguments and balancing a tight budget; one day, the youngest walks into the kitchen and thanks her mom for doing the laundry. The phone rings and a friend from twenty years ago calls to thank you for the advice and encouragement you offered the last time you spoke – and you can't even remember the conversation that changed his life.

The second letter to the Corinthians reminds us that we are clay jars, ordinary signs of the extraordinary God: "But we have this treasure in clay jars, so that it may be made clear that this extraordinary power belongs to God and does not come from us" (2 Corinthians 4:7). Jesus himself comes among us as a clay jar, fully God and fully human, taking on our humanity in the ordinary way, born in a small town to a carpenter and a virgin. When Jesus rises from the dead, his body is a clay jar that carries the power of God to bring us new life. Every moment of his life was not as significant as his death and resurrection, but every moment contributed to who he became in the extraordinary moment that he chose to suffer and die for us. In the work, effort, joy and suffering of our daily lives, we have glimpses of the greatness of God. These glimpses give us the courage to say yes to simply showing up for our lives so God can make them extraordinary.

QUESTIONS FOR REFLECTION

1. When has God asked you to follow him? When have you said yes? When have you hesitated or refused? What do those moments look like, feel like, sound like? How do they change you?

2. When have you had glimpses of what God is doing in and around you? How and with whom do you share those stories? Who shares their stories with you?

3. How do you discern God's call in your daily life? What activities, relationships or prayers seem to work in helping you arrive at decisions? How does the process of arriving at a decision feel for you? Are you more comfortable with the discerning or with the final decision?

CHAPTER 11

From the Stable
to the Cross

And a voice came from heaven, "You are my Son, the Beloved; with you I am well pleased."

~ *Mark 1:11*

Adam and Eve are the only people in creation whose stories begin without infancy and childhood. When Jesus is born among us, he arrives in the usual way: tiny, naked, unadorned. He lives the spousal meaning of his body from his birth in the stable to his death on the cross. And then he rises from the dead and shows us that living the spousal meaning of the body will lead to resurrection – both his and ours. We share in God's life in and through our bodies for every moment of our existence, not just when we cross the threshold into adulthood.

The second half of *Theology of the Body* is an application of John Paul's foundational ideas to marriage. It is an important application (especially in the realm of sexual expression, which will be discussed more fully in Chapter 13 of this book), but I have come to think of it as a first application, rather than the only application of John Paul's ideas about being human. He acknowledges that those called to celibacy also share in the spousal meaning of the body. Of course, we all begin life called to celibacy. And many people called to marriage find themselves living celibacy again at some point in their lives, due to widowhood, divorce, illness or other exceptional circumstances.

As disciples of Jesus, then, we are called to be and become fully human in every stage of our growth. We can learn about the spousal meaning of the body, in our experience and with language, as that becomes a possibility. We can connect our story to the God story and act in ways that change our hearts and change the world. No one is too young or too old to live the spousal meaning of the body. We just have to be attentive to *how* we can live it out from the crib to the classroom, the car to the casket. And all along the way, we live out the meaning of our bodies, with other people doing likewise.

Born in a Stable

The birth of Jesus is one of the most powerful God stories. It is God's story and it is our story. Mary's was an unexpected pregnancy; Joseph might be the most famous stepdad in history. Jesus is born in a stable at Bethlehem (likely not Mary's first choice of birthing locations), and then this holy little family takes refuge in Egypt. Our God spoke tentative first words, learned the language of his parents, fell down trying to take first steps. He played with his food, imitated Mary cooking and followed Joseph around, picking up stones. Maybe he had Mary's eyes, and repeated everything Joseph said.

Infancy and childhood are not merely times to be quickly passed through on the way to becoming an image of God. Every stage of our humanity is an image of God, a glimpse of divinity, a moment where we can encounter God within ourselves. The vulnerability of a baby reminds us that the power of God is not only present in human ability, knowledge and authority. Childhood is the embodiment of discovery, the highpoint of wonder and awe. God is present and empowered in us when we are unable, when we have no formal education and no job. Among other miracles of these stages of life, infancy and childhood are signs of our creation for relationships of interdependence.

This book is not going to be read by infants or children but by their parents, grandparents, aunts, uncles, pastors, teachers and friends. As adults, we reflect on our own beginnings, on the early experiences of our lives, so we can learn about who we have been, who we are, and who God is calling us to become. As those who love and care for children, we reflect on our experiences with children to recognize what we offer to them and what they have offered to us. Our reflection will be particular, grounded in the details of our experiences.

When Siobhan and Jelani were expecting their third baby, they were surrounded by a calm anticipation of birth. That changed at 33 weeks, however, when the baby's growth seemed to have stopped. Tests shed little light on what was happening, and with nervous anxiety, the family waited for a scheduled birthday by Caesarean section, prepared for the worst but hoping for a healthy baby. When Michael was born, he was diagnosed with muscular dystrophy. For a moment, Siobhan was flooded with tears, feeling devastation for the suffering her son would face in his lifetime. But as she held him, she felt God loving him through her and knew that Michael needed her love and support much more than her sympathy. Weeks later, the whole family gathered around Michael on the floor one evening after his bath. All the smiles they had poured out on him were returned as he offered them his first of a lifetime of smiles.

Benoit is three months old. He's been colicky for eleven of his twelve weeks on the planet and his parents haven't had more than two hours of consecutive sleep since his birth. The sound of his crying makes their blood pressure rise and their hearts break. And his sister, Brianne, wants them to get rid of the "cryin' baby." The only thing Benoit is offering is himself – to be cared for. Several times in each very long twenty-four-hour day, he falls asleep on the chest of one of his parents. His parents are fed by his need for them, by the perfection of his tiny nose and by the sound of his short, quiet breaths. That moment is the moment that allows them to pour themselves out for him for the rest of the day.

Annika was born on the hottest night of summer in a small-town hospital. Every year, the classes of kindergarten students are getting smaller. Annika was baby number six this year, and a universal source of celebration in town because she is the first baby number six in three years. And there are two more babies due before the end of the year. Everywhere Annika goes, people are smiling – because she's a baby and because her very body is a sign proclaiming that life in the small town is still possible.

I remember confessing once that I kept falling asleep when I was praying. The priest gently laughed, saying, "What makes you think God loves you less when you are sleeping?" I was kind of annoyed at him for laughing until, years later, I sat in the rocking chair holding one of my own sleeping babies. I am so much more aware of the depth of my love for them when they are sleeping. Each tiny, barely audible breath a reminder that their lives go on while they rest. The fists formed in pre-sleep crying relaxing into open palms. The hands that will drive go-carts, build sandcastles, pick dandelions.

Casey was six when she was adopted into a stable family after years of foster care. She was angry and defensive. She had had some nice foster families and some not so nice ones, but the constant moving made her skeptical that she could trust anyone other than herself. One night before bed, Casey and her mom were saying prayers, asking blessings for all the people they had met that day. Casey asked to pray for Annie, too. After the prayer, her mom asked her who Annie was. Casey replied, "Annie's my best friend. She knew me when I was a baby, and she has come with me to every house. She would hold my hand when someone yelled at me and play with me when the other kids wouldn't. She's imaginary, but God can bless her too, right?"

Tim had been told "no" three times when he slipped the race car into his pocket at the toy store. The thrill was electric. His ten-year-old body was almost shaking in the car all the way home. When they got there, he rushed off to his room to play with it. He managed to keep the car a secret for a few days, until his mom came into his room to tell him sup-per was ready and saw the car lined up beside the others. "After supper," she said, calmly, "we will be going back to the store and you will be pay-ing for that car with the birthday money you were saving. And we'll be putting the car in the box for the kids at the shelter." It took Tim a long time to forgive his Mom for "humiliating" him. When he was working part-time as an assistant manager at a grocery store during university, though, a parent came in with a timid little girl and an opened pack of gum. It took more than a little effort for him to refrain from grinning the whole time he listened to her apology.

When my daughter Robyn was four, she looked up from her col-ouring and asked if I could feel God inside me. I think I was gutting a turkey at the time. I stopped, moving my energy from my hands to my heart, and answered, "Yes, sometimes I can feel God inside me." She went back to her colouring and said, matter-of-factly, "I feel God inside me all the time." Smiling, I asked, "What does God feel like, inside you?" She looked at me with confusion: "Like God, Mommy." Of course. This got me thinking about when exactly it was that I stopped feeling God inside me all the time. And every so often, I try to remember to ask her how God is doing inside her.

Lost in the Temple

Most of Jesus' early life is not recorded in the Bible. From his presentation in the temple to the beginning of his public ministry in baptism, we hear two things. First, we know that the "child grew and became strong, filled with wisdom; and the favour of God was upon him" (Luke 2:40). And then we have the story about Jesus in the temple in Jerusalem.

I love to imagine the scene. Mary and Joseph are travelling with a large group to Jerusalem to celebrate the Passover. As they prepare to return home, they assume that their son is with the other young boys, under the watchful eye of neighbours, aunts and uncles, grandparents. After a day's travel, Mary catches up with Joseph, saying something like "How's Jesus doing?" Joseph looks at her and says, "I thought he was with you." They calmly begin to ask around. The calm turns to panic. *We have been entrusted with the Son of God and we lost him!* They turn around and head back to Jerusalem. For three days, they look. There is no amber alert system, no television monitors to flash his picture on. They can't track his cell phone.

Perhaps they go to the temple when they are on the verge of giving up, to make a desperate plea for God to intervene, and there, sitting in the temple, asking questions of the teachers, is Jesus. Mary says, "Child, why have you treated us like this? Look, your father and I have been searching for you in great anxiety." Jesus is both Godly and typically teen in his response: "Why were you searching for me? Did you not know that I must be in my Father's house?" (The adult Jesus might have mentioned to Mary where he was going.) Mary and Joseph don't understand that Jesus is already growing in an awareness of his own call. Despite the absence of sin, the holy family, like all families, faces conflict, misunderstanding and confusion. And, after the whole thing is resolved, Jesus returns to Nazareth with his family and grows "in divine and human favour" (Luke 2:41-52).

Jamar spent his whole life fending for himself. His parents did not make much money and their marriage was always tense. They tried their best to love him, but they were always working. In an effort to get their attention, he tried to push every boundary they gave him. He used his outside voice inside, got detention on purpose, started dating girls he knew they wouldn't like. Eventually, he realized that his parents weren't going to take notice. In his last year of high school, Mrs. Alley noticed him. She noticed a strong young man with some exceptionally good problem-solving skills. Mrs. Alley recommended that Jamar apply for a scholarship, helped him with the application, got him involved in some new activities. After years of feeling alone, he started to feel connected, inspired and capable.

When Ben was fourteen, he was excited to learn that he was the only Grade 9 student to make the high school basketball team – until he realized this meant his best friend would not be on the team. When he went home that night to tell his parents, he had decided that he simply wouldn't join the team if Jonah wasn't on it. Ben was not interested in listening to his parents until his dad caught his attention while they were shooting baskets in the driveway after supper. Ben's dad explained that growing up requires difficult decisions that are sometimes painful for us and for other people. They talked for a long time. Ben realized that Jonah was going to be disappointed that he wasn't on the team whether Ben played on the team or not. Ben could play basketball and be Jonah's best friend, even if it was hard.

Jana has two sets of parents who love her. Her mom and dad were young when she was born and they never married. Before she was three, both her parents had married other people and Jana had a happy life going between the two homes. She had great relationships with her step-parents and everyone agreed she was happy, well-adjusted and healthy, despite the bullying that plagued her through middle school. When she turned sixteen, however, she started dating a guy who was twenty and addicted to meth. Both sets of parents tried everything they could to discourage the relationship, to stop Jana from using. Their best efforts were unsuccessful, and by nineteen, their daughter was addicted to the same drug. When she checked into rehab, she still had four parents trying their best to love her. Jana's not sure she is going to be able to endure the withdrawal, let alone face her parents when she's clean. Her parents are trying to separate their worth from their daughter's choices: they know that good kids and good parents face hard realities, but they are still trying to blame themselves.

Lynne was raised in the church but stopped going and believing somewhere in her teens. As a young adult, she was a good person, working, studying and volunteering. But one day she woke up and felt sick of her life, lost in the endless possibility of choices and inspired by none of them. She made an appointment with Sr. Lucy, who ran the women's shelter where Lynne volunteered. When she walked into Sr. Lucy's office, she sat down on the desk and asked, "Is it possible to be a prodigal daughter?"

One of the gifts of the teen years is the growing ability to understand who we are and who we want to become. As we grow into young adulthood, we *begin* to appreciate why our parents taught us to brush our teeth, take showers and wear clean underwear. We *begin* to have a sense of what our gifts are and how we might use them. Often, we get lost, and hopefully, we get found. Adolescence and emerging adulthood also image God: a God who holds tension, endures ridicule, cares what we think about him. Our God is a God who seeks us when we are lost and who celebrates the beauty of even the awkward stages of growth.

Cana and Beyond

I love the story of Jesus and Mary at the wedding at Cana. Jesus is an adult, a grown man, and when the wine runs out at the wedding banquet, Mary asks Jesus to do something. I have often wondered what experiences they had shared before that day that made Mary think Jesus could do something. And they have this wonderful exchange, mother and son. Mary tells Jesus that there is no wine. Jesus asks her why that is their problem. Then he adds, almost as an aside, "My hour has not yet come" (John 2:4). He says he's not going to do anything, but Mary acts like she did not hear him, telling the servants to follow Jesus' instructions. The beginning of Jesus' ministry takes place as two unnamed people begin their lives together. This is the first public miracle, the first sign of who Jesus is and will be. Jesus resists the first request and then offers himself with Mary's encouragement. And his public ministry begins.

Adulthood arrives gradually, as we live the experiences of life: moving away from home, finishing school, starting a first job, saying vows, welcoming children, facing the death of a parent, losing a job, or living with illness. Some people can pinpoint the moment they grew up; others wake up and wonder how it happened. We often treat adulthood as though we have arrived at a point when our growing has stopped. But our growth does not stop when we reach adulthood, it just becomes less visible in the body. We resist seeing this stage of growth in the body in part because our culture has mistakenly associated aging with decline instead of growth.

When I began working in ministry, I was very blessed by colleagues who were twice and three times my age. They enjoyed teasing me when I related newlywed stories, shared parenting wisdom with me, envied the height of my heels. I would listen to them, love them and exclaim, "I can't wait to be fifty!" And they would laugh at me, and tell me not to wish my youth away. But I'm not wishing it away – I am just excited to grow older, to gain the wisdom, confidence and patience that emerge with time, grace and life experience. Perhaps it is youthful idealism that I am forcing you to suffer with me. Perhaps I will recant this section in the book I write just after moving into a nursing home, but somehow, I doubt it.

I'm just so convinced that adulthood is more than the inevitable grindstone, the space of life between the so-called glory days of youth and retirement. Adulthood is our continued growing towards God, the maturing of familial relationships, the establishment of relationships of our choosing, the space where childhood play and adolescent discovery give way to seasons of fragrant blooming and winter's cold rest alike. Adulthood is our chance to practise and play, to do and do again, to love and forgive. Our culture has very few rites of passage for adults. The last cultural rite of passage is marriage, if people choose it. Children are celebrated, but parenthood is not supported in Western culture the way it might be, and then it is the children's accomplishments that are celebrated until retirement. Faith offers us the liturgical year, a beautiful way to celebrate lifelong growth, begun in infancy, lived through childhood and into adulthood, where we settle and make a life for ourselves.

Each feast is a celebration, each season of revisiting once again a place we have been before – familiar and also altogether new.

Inri is a journalist. She travels not as a tourist, but as an aspiring local, a storyteller. This year, she is working as a foreign correspondent in the Middle East, writing the stories of unmarried women across religious and national boundaries. She wouldn't put it in these words, but she was made for ordinary time. Even in a country far from home, she loves getting up early, watching the sun rise, reading the paper, remembering the events of the day from the years that have gone by. Today is the thirteenth anniversary of her mother's remission from bone cancer. When she looked in the mirror this morning, Inri saw her mother's face: the laugh lines, the bits of grey hair sneaking out from under the colour. The fear of illness sits in her throat, a little stronger than last year, but with less intensity than the years right after the diagnosis. And the sun came up those mornings, too, with bright possibility and new stories waiting to be told.

Olivia has been waiting on Dave to be ready for the move for about a year. Last time, it took three years from the time she said it needed to happen until he was willing to put the house up for sale. They knew when they married that her work would require it, but they didn't know then how hard Dave found moving. In their fifteen years of marriage, Olivia has learned that she needs to wait for Dave to see what she sees instead of flipping on the lights in the dead of night. Dave has learned to appreciate Olivia's foresight, her gentle pressure and his own need to understand for himself. The first years of their marriage were filled with arguments, resentment and forceful attempts to make each other change. While they can still argue with passion, they have found a season of peace in learning to wait on each other, which makes the moves much more manageable for both of them.

Henry thinks being a grandparent is God's way of thanking him for parenting. His son, Will, and daughter-in-law, Meg, just brought home a third baby, a surprise addition to their two teenage boys. Henry holds the tiny pink bundle and smiles as Will sends the boys to clean their rooms before they go out to a movie, and warns them not to wake their mom. Henry will make dinner. He remembers teaching his son to hold a knife. He remembers learning to cook himself. He doesn't quite remember when he got so tired, but he is grateful that Will and Meg were so willing to let him come and live with them. The house is always full – of kids, noise and activity – but Henry can still show up for breakfast. His famous "look" gets the boys out to shovel the snow faster than any other tactic. Age is softening his edges, and he is unlearning his addiction to doing everything. He never thought he could enjoy receiving quite so much, but these grandkids are teaching him how much he missed with his own kids.

Sr. Celine just attended the funeral of one of her dearest friends. They joined the order together, went to the same novitiate, taught at the same school for twenty years. These days are difficult; it seems like they lose another sister every month and they stopped accepting new sisters years ago. This reality was unimaginable when she started this journey. But last week, while Sr. Celine spent a day in a high school assisting with the drama production, she sat with several young girls. They were as vibrant and hopeful as ever, overflowing with the same strange blend of idealism and fear she remembers feeling at that age. For a few moments, she felt the energy and urgency of her own youth.

Growth begins at the moment of our conception, as cells divide and multiply, organizing and forming into the various parts of the body. When a baby grows in the safety of the womb, the umbilical cord and placenta develop to nurture the baby during this stage of life. Those parts of the mother's body grow old and die as the baby is born into life in the world. We grow baby teeth and lose them. Our hair grows and we cut it off. We reach sexual maturity, trading in the childish traits of our bodies for those of adulthood. As we age, normal human growth includes the development of laugh lines, the greying of hair and the wearing of our joints. These changes cannot be contrasted with the growth of youth, as though one is good and the other is not. Growth in every stage involves a bit of suffering, a measure of dying to the old and welcoming the new. If we age with God's grace, we let go of the idea that the changed reality will necessarily be an improvement on all fronts when we compare it with the previous one.

Adulthood is the slow transformation of our bodies and our souls. It is season after season of showing up for our lives, recognizing the lessons of the past while we love the newness of the present and anticipate the future. Adulthood is an image of the God who chooses to keep loving us, who is constantly attentive to the creation he has long known, who continually bears and brings forth our very lives, new and old in every season. Our God is a God who cares tenderly, who laughs until he has laugh lines, whose life and work is impressed in the look of his hands.

Take this Cup

When Jesus goes to pray in the garden at Gethsemane, he knows his death is coming. He doesn't get the privilege of aging, the time he might have hoped for to love his disciples, to answer their questions, to calm their fears. He brings some of his friends with him, begging them to stay awake and pray with him. Alone in the garden, he cries out to God, saying, "My Father, if it is possible, let this cup pass from me." And as he prays through his fear; he faces it: "My Father, if this cannot pass unless I drink it, your will be done" (Matthew 26:39, 42). He goes through the persecution and crucifixion surrounded by disciples, followers and friends who cannot take the cup from him. Even his mother cannot take it away.

The traditional statue of the *Pieta* depicts Mary holding the body of Jesus after the crucifixion. This image is a profound witness of the experience of suffering and death – for a mother and a Son. As we are called, in the spousal meaning of the body, to give ourselves away, the final call we will all face is to let go of our very lives, to let go into dying, and even death. And how many of us will sit in our own Gethsemane, asking God for another way, a different cup?

My grandpa taught us to play cribbage. He came for drives through the fields and told us stories about how the farm had changed over his lifetime. As I went through grade school, he moved into the nursing home. He let go of his mobility and his home. As I married and welcomed my first baby, he let go of his eyesight and his hearing. As I acquired the gifts and blessings of youth, he was letting them go, one by one, with open hands. He gave our family the gift of letting go of his life's acquisitions with grace. When Grandpa died, I reached for the leathery comfort of his hand for the last time. As I sat with his body, I realized that I had witnessed his Gethsemane and its grace over twenty years. And I prayed that I would be able to live mine like he lived his.

I met Ella when she was in remission from an aggressive cancer that claims the lives of most of its victims. She was bright and beautiful, passionate and patient. I didn't get to know her in the height of her health. I never met her children and I didn't get to go to her funeral when the cancer came back. In her last weeks, she asked me to come to the hospital to pray with her. When I walked into the room and sat beside her in silent prayer, she thanked me for being one of the people who didn't need her to be sad about dying. It was a consequence of the length of our friendship that I could let her go with the same ease with which she had sung her way into my life. It was one of the most profound privileges of my life that she shared with me her moment of letting go. She had been fighting the cancer so hard and she was so tired. In a moment of grace, she shared the source of her hope: "Whether I live or die, I will live."

When I began my work in ministry, I was twenty-three. Within a year, I was frustrated that the challenges were so big and it was so difficult to see any movement towards change. The idea of something taking ten or twenty years to accomplish was outside of my experience, because ten years before I had been planning sleepovers and handing in grammar lessons. Twenty years before, I had just turned three. In that first year of ministry, I realized that many of the things I care most about will require more people than just me to address. The issues, situations and people that I am passionate about will take more love, time and attention than I could hope to offer in the longest possible duration of my life. I found this realization freeing, in terms of both my life and my death. The work I do and the life I live are not mine. They never were. My life and work have always been a *participation* in God's life, my offering for whatever time I have here.

The wisdom of life is that we return to the place where we began: a blessed and embodied interdependence that allows us to share our solitude until we surrender it to God himself. From our infancy through to our death, we are offered opportunities to give ourselves to God and each other by simply being present for our lives. When the heavens open and we hear the voice of God, we want to hear what Jesus heard: "This is my child, the Beloved; with you I am well pleased."

QUESTIONS FOR REFLECTION

1. What have you loved about the different ages and stages of your life? What has been challenging about each stage? How do the experiences of those stages affect the way you live now?

2. Who have you shared life with over the years? How has their growth affected your own? What gifts of growth have you been able to share with others?

3. If you were to write your own obituary now, what would it say? At the end of your life on earth, how might God describe the gift you have offered with your life? What would you need to change now and for the years to come so that you are the gift you want to be? The gift God is calling you to be?

CHAPTER 12

To Whom Can We Go?

"This is my body, which is given for you."

~ Luke 22:19

In the Gospel of John, after many people have started to follow Jesus, things get messy. As he is teaching, he insists, after repeated questioning, "Very truly, I tell you, unless you eat the flesh of the Son of Man and drink his blood, you have no life in you" (John 6:53). Some followers fall away because this teaching is just too difficult. Jesus, knowing that some people are leaving, turns to the disciples, his most faithful followers, and says, "Do you also wish to go away?" Simon Peter responds freely, "Lord, to whom can we go? You have the words of eternal life. We have come to believe and know that you are the Holy One of God" (John 6:67-69).

God's desire for us is abundant life. Peter's response shows that he understands what is at stake here. Peter does not say he finds Jesus' teaching easy, so he'll stick around for today. He and other disciples likely struggled to understand what Jesus was saying and how they were supposed to live it out. Yet Peter puts the matter on a different plane when he says, "To whom can we go?" His answer is the key to how we live the spousal meaning of the body when self-giving stops being effortless. We root ourselves in the One we know and believe to be the Holy One of God: Jesus. Like Peter, we know that Jesus offers us life, even when we cannot see how.

In the world, adulthood arrives on a birthday, when all of a sudden we can sign a contract, enlist in the military, get married, and vote, among other things. Whether or not a person is ready, the law declares them responsible for themselves. Spiritually, maturity is not a given of any age; it arrives when the circumstances of our lives call it out of us and we have the courage to respond.

Kim's childhood was over when the flood hit and took everything. She had to stop going to school at fourteen and help her parents earn enough money to survive. She learned that God doesn't take away suffering, but he can refine us in it. When she faced breast cancer at twenty-three, her spiritual maturity kept her from being angry and rooted her in hope. In flood recovery and illness alike, her body carried the struggles and took its rest in faith. Lane was fifty-seven when he realized that the catechism of his childhood was no longer sufficient. He had been content to allow God to dwell in simple answers to simple questions and not think too much about God. Lane sinned as he wanted to and used confession to wipe the slate clean. But he kept waking in the night, feeling guilty about the affair, his conscience eating at him. Over the past year, the sacrament of Reconciliation had stopped making him feel better. He had to choose to end the affair and face the consequences of being honest with himself and his wife, or he had to give up on God and feel his misery as his body physically resisted sleep.

When we grow into an adult spirituality, we discover that love and faithfulness are choices. We fall in love effortlessly; we stay in love with the effort of putting another person before ourselves. We can go to church, follow the rules, be good people, but those things in themselves may not be enough. We find a mature spirituality when the external actions become integrated with our hearts, when we seek to be changed by going to church, when we struggle to love the discipline of the rules, when we face our brokenness and still believe, with God, that we are good. The growth of a mature spirituality takes place in the body, both as we are refined internally and have more space inside ourselves for others. Our adult growth is slow and less visible than in our childhood, but it plays out in the body when we hold the hand of a teenage girl giving birth to a baby that she will place for adoption. Our growth emerges when we still have a place at the table for an adult child who is making destructive decisions. We live into God's capacity to love when we call a friend who is going through a divorce and try to provide support. We choose the vulnerability of faith when we go into a war zone without weapons, to bear witness to the possibility of peace. We grow into our faith when we stop trying to tell God what to do and how to be and start being attentive to what God is doing and calling us to become.

Mature faith knows the discomfort and suffering required by sacrifice, even while it seeks to hold onto a child-like wonder, generosity and joy. Alongside Peter and the other disciples, when things get difficult, we are not bound by Jesus or enslaved by faith. Jesus allows us the freedom to walk away and the dignity of choosing to stay, even when it is tough.

Life is messy. We have competing demands on our time, attention, resources and abilities. We work with varying levels of health and dysfunction in ourselves and in others. Living the spousal meaning of the body does not reduce everything to a simplistic and potentially dangerous selflessness that disregards our own needs and always concedes to the demands of others. When we live out the spousal meaning of the body as adults, we become attentive to the dignity of humanity and we enter into our experience with reverence for God's presence there. We practise making meaning with as truthful an understanding as we can, gathering information from our experience and that of others. We form values with intention and make every attempt to connect the values we hold in faith with the way we live and act. We learn from our mistakes, practise forgiveness, hold fast to hope, and rejoice in the moments of grace and new life. And all this theory plays out in the stories of our lives.

Ana is a single parent to three children. While the kids are playing and doing homework, she is going over her budget. Things have been tight lately and she is saving up to ensure she will have enough money to buy Christmas presents for the kids in addition to contributing something to the parish food drive. Then the phone rings. Her brother has recently been released from prison. He's a good kid and his arrest and sentence for impaired driving were a wake-up call, spurring him to get the help he needs to deal with his alcoholism. He finally got a job, and has been doing really well. But, he explains, his power bill was higher than he expected, because of the recent cold snap and the poor insulation in his apartment. He has lied in the past and her attempts to help have fuelled his addiction, but sometimes he's telling the truth. Her shoulders creep towards her ears and her hands cling tightly around her pen. How does she protect her own heart from being broken and respect her brother's dignity? How is she called to support herself, her kids and her brother, with her limited financial resources and with quality time, attention and encouragement?

Fr. Cary is trying to work on a homily on a Friday afternoon when the phone rings. His long-time friend has been recently widowed and is wondering if they could maybe get together tonight. Fr. Cary had really been hoping for a quiet night at home. He has been working too much and it is starting to take a toll on his patience. He snapped at the parish assistant again this afternoon. She was just trying to make his life easier when she interrupted him to remind him that he had promised to visit a sick parishioner on his way home for the night. These kinds of decisions never seem to get any easier, even after twelve years of priesthood. He leans back in his chair, taking a deep breath and feeling his exhaustion in his jaw. Is he called to offer himself to his friend, to reschedule the stop at the hospital, or to protect his ability to offer himself through the demands of weekend ministry by choosing to stay home and go to bed early?

Geoff spends most of his days caring for Lina, his wife of thirty-seven years, who had a stroke last year. Together, they have faced many challenges: a long struggle with infertility, the moves and demands associated with her career in policing, his two layoffs and subsequent bouts with depression, and the adoption and raising of two children. Geoff has long been aware of the sacrifices Lina has made over their life together in supporting him through depression, and he made similar sacrifices to support her police work, but caring for her while watching her struggle so hard for every word is almost too much. He is feeling guilty because every day, he is tempted to walk away. His feet and hands feel so heavy. How is he called to care for the both of them?

Living the spousal meaning of the body does not mean we will always make the right decisions or our actions will be understood and appreciated by those around us. Disciples enter deeply into these moments, knowing that they matter, seeking grace in the mess of it, and desiring to be refined by both the successes and the failures. Usually, grace emerges more clearly in hindsight than it does in the mess. When his friend calls on Monday to thank him for sharing his quiet night in with a favourite movie, Fr. Cary knows he helped and got the rest he needed. Ana still doesn't know if she's going to have the money for the Christmas gifts, but giving twenty dollars to her brother when she needed it herself was her disciplined choice to have hope in him. She has resolved not to beat herself up by fixating on whether she should have given him money. Geoff has arranged for their children to come and spend a day with Lina once every two weeks so he can see a counsellor and attend a support group for caregivers. Even though he is finding the demands of life overwhelming, when Lina fights for one more word or gets more movement back in one finger, he sees the grace of his work and hers.

Fr. Cary reads the Scriptures regularly, prays the liturgy of the hours, and believes that his priesthood is a gift to him and to the people he serves. But the disciplines and guides of the church that he studied in the seminary don't tell him whether he should take a night off or work eighty hours this week. He has to discern that call, seek to understand his experiences and continually develop values that allow him to serve God faithfully and participate in grace. Ana has visited the prisoner, cared for the sick and lived with the poor in loving her brother, but the Bible does not tell her whether she should give her brother money on Tuesday. Geoff knows that he vowed to be faithful in sickness as well as health, but that vow doesn't tell him how to live it out. Mature spirituality takes us beyond the expectation that someone else will take responsibility for the decisions that give shape to our lives and our souls. Practising our faith will help us to develop the habits that make holy decisions easier, but following the rules alone will not sustain us. We have to be changed by the God we worship. In the most challenging moments, we face our solitude and offer ourselves to God in the shades of grey that we might be transformed by his mercy, compassion and presence.

I have cried out to God with anger, frustration, grief or despair on several significant occasions in my life. In each of these moments, in the words of a friend, the silence of prayer, or the release of tears, I have heard Jesus say to me, "Do you also wish to go away?"

When I was looking for a church that perfectly embodied *my* beliefs about God.

When my marriage was difficult.

When a priest I trusted was arrested for abusing a child.

Peter's perspective shifted my perspective. I doubt I will ever find every teaching of the church easy to learn and practise. My spouse is not a problem for me to solve, but a person for me to love. The priesthood is not immune from sin. And God still chooses to love this messy, broken world, and me in it. When I say that I "believe in" Jesus, I don't mean I have an intellectual conviction that he lived and died and rose again (although I do have that conviction). To "believe in" Jesus means I am in a relationship with Jesus, a relationship that matters more than my being right, comfortable and justified all of the time. "To whom can we go? You have the words of eternal life." I choose to stay in relationship with Jesus because he gave me life and shares it with me. He has walked with me through the challenges and shares my desire to create a world where churches invite us to grow, marriages are life-giving and no one suffers abuse.

Just after we confirmed our first pregnancy, my husband moved across the country ahead of me to start a new job. Near the end of the three months of living apart, I was sick and tired of being sick and tired. One day, I arrived in body at Mass, but my mind was wandering all over. *If I see one more set of stairs to climb, I think my legs will fall off. I miss Marc. Why didn't anyone tell me that such a small baby could make me feel so rotten? I'm never going to finish my thesis....* When my attention was finally jolted back to the present moment, the priest had lifted the host, and I heard, "This is my Body, given up for you." I looked down at the tiny bump growing above my belt and thought, *All right already. I get it. I'll stop complaining.* And I started to smile, even laugh a little, as I looked at Jesus looking back at me. *I can choose to find joy in the midst of this.*

I am often guilty of making faith and life too serious. Mature faith acknowledges that our lives are significant, challenging and holy ground, but it also finds the joy. When the world has the impression that church sucks the fun out of life, we have communicated to them by the way we carry our bodies that God is a killjoy. There is no doubt that life is hard, but it is also beautiful. We are called to celebrate beauty, laugh deeply, toss up our hands in the midst of suffering and notice what is spectacular about life.

Lise is the life of every party. She loves to visit with people, always remembers the details of the last conversation, and can invite participation from even the most reluctant characters. Whether she's dancing up a storm at a salsa class, serving up a fabulous meal at her house or delivering her latest research in a conference paper, people are always surprised to discover that she is a Christian. She gets up at six every day to pray, and she throws an annual New Year's party that everyone hopes to attend. She loves to go dancing but she doesn't go home with anyone except her roommate at the end of the night.

Carter comes from a family that expects excellence. He never got rewarded for bringing home good report cards. It never occurred to him to have a house-warming party when he bought his house. He saved his money and made a purchase, because that's what responsible people do. Last year, he had a performance review at work where he received great feedback about his work as a manager with his company. His boss, however, noted that Carter rarely offers positive feedback or encouragement to the people he works with. It had never occurred to Carter to praise or thank people who were doing their jobs well. So for the last year, Carter has been experimenting with encouragement, gratitude and celebration. He has noticed even better performance by some of his staff members. But the biggest change he has experienced is how much more he enjoys his work and the people he works with. And his wife and his kids aren't complaining about the experiment, either.

Fr. Emmanuel is one of the quietest pastors his parishioners have ever had. But he is also the funniest. His homilies are short and always include several big laughs. When people are dying, Fr. Emmanuel walks the line between caring for the grieving with his quiet presence and his usual prayer of thanksgiving to God for the gift of great and abundant food at times of tragedy. After forty years of priesthood, he describes and addresses issues with clarity and then puts on his rain boots and jumps in the biggest puddles, daring others to join him.

Redemption is not a magic button that God pushes at some point between our baptism and our arrival at the gates of heaven. Redemption is what happens, moment by moment and day by day, when we manage not to say the first nasty thing that comes to our minds when we feel hurt. We become more fully human when we just do the dishes without spending the whole time begrudging the person whose turn it was. We grow in holiness when we get up in the night to soothe a crying child or head to the hospital to anoint someone who is dying. We live out the spousal meaning of our body when we refuse to allow road rage to take us over, when we make hope-filled assumptions about the actions of others, when we choose to ask for what we need instead of playing games with people. Gradually, with years of practice at receiving God's grace, we become better disciples – and better sons and daughters, siblings, friends, neighbours, spouses, priests and community members.

QUESTIONS FOR REFLECTION

1. When have you been tempted by Jesus' question: "Do you also want to go away?" Have you ever gone? If so, what brought you back? If not, why have you chosen to stay?

2. When is self-giving easy for you? When is it especially hard? Whose gifts of self do you receive most easily? Whose gifts are hardest to receive?

3. When have you lived sacrifice in your body, felt its demands in aching muscles, longed for physical rest? Who is blessed by the sacrifices you live in your body and soul?

CHAPTER 13

A Seal on Your Heart

Set me as a seal upon your heart,
as a seal upon your arm;
for love is strong as death, passion fierce as the grave.
Its flashes are flashes of fire, a raging flame.

~ *Song of Songs* 8:6

Given the attention that *Theology of the Body* has received in the realm of sexuality, this book would not be complete without giving some attention to human sexuality. John Paul has situated sex in the context of human love, as a part of the self-giving to which we are called as God's people. He reflects on marriage and sexuality at length in the second half of the work. But, in the last chapter, he also says that "the term 'theology of the body' goes far beyond the content of the reflections presented here" (TOB 133:1).

Sexuality, like the spousal meaning of the body, is a constant in our experience of being human. Baby boys get called "sir" and "little man" and girls are "princess" and "pretty little one." Whether or not we agree with the way our culture responds to and shapes sexual difference is secondary to the basic biological fact that sexual difference means that every relationship of our lives has a sexual dimension.

The fact that our bodies are male and female is a sign of our creation for relationships. Signs and symbols are not limiting and final – they are expansive. Our human capacity for relationships that allow us to procreate (with God) is also a sign of our desire for communion at all levels, for friendship and family, for collaboration and belonging. This is how it is possible for John Paul to say that we also live out the spousal meaning of the body when we are celibate.

Sexuality, then, is the fire in us that draws us out of ourselves into relationships with others. It is the longing we experience in solitude that allows us to celebrate experiences of unity. Sexuality is closely linked to human spirituality. Both have physical dimensions in the way they are lived out in the body. We are male and female; we touch and need to be touched; we navigate relationships with attentiveness to the passions, desires and sensitivities of others. We pray with words and actions; we worship in churches and in nature; we cry out to God with faith that God hears us. At the same time, both sexuality and spirituality have immaterial dimensions. We cannot physically measure the longing of loneliness, the joy of consolation, or the connection between friends, grandparents and grandchildren, or lovers.

The flames of sexuality and spirituality have been lit in our bodies and in our souls. The author of the Song of Songs expresses the longing of love, saying, "Set me as a seal upon your heart, as a seal upon your arm." Some people read this long song spiritually, as the human longing for God, and others read it sexually, as the human desire for sexual love. It is both. Our longing for human love of every kind is an expression of our spiritual restlessness and longing for God. We desire to be the beloved, to be impressed upon the hearts of others. That desire, both spiritual and sexual, is only ever satisfied in incomplete and fleeting ways in our human experience. Every so often, when I go to Mass, I am able to really focus on what is happening. The music draws me in, the readings and homily are just what I needed to hear, and the Eucharist nourishes me, giving me a new energy to live faith when I leave. But then, just as tenuously as it all came together, it falls apart and I feel lost again. And much more often, my prayer and worship does not work out perfectly and I am left longing for more of God. My marriage has affirmed that sexuality is much the same as spirituality. Occasionally, everything falls into place and everything goes beautifully. And then life happens and there is an interruption and we are left longing for more of each other, and more of God, once again. When God created us, he put a piece of himself in us, a piece of divinity that will not be satisfied until we are fully united with God.

In *Theology of the Body*, John Paul holds onto an ancient understanding of *eros*, a word for love that is the root of the more contemporary and commonly used "erotic." The word once referred to our desire for all that is true and good and beautiful (TOB 47:2). Truth, goodness and beauty exist in our sexuality, but not only there. Sex matters and it doesn't matter, depending on how intently its passion strikes us and our ability to find a way to participate in truth, goodness and beauty. The longing we feel deeply in our bodies is intended to be a gift, not a curse.

In talking about how we live out the spousal meaning of the body throughout our lives, it is tempting to follow the traditional separation of marriage and celibacy. I will resist that temptation because our pursuit of the true, good and beautiful is not limited by our marital state. Across our vocational identities and over the course of our lives, we all share the same spousal meaning of the body. That objective truth of our humanity is lived out in the subjective particularities of our lives, one of which is whether we are called to marriage or single life. But that is not the only particularity that matters. Every marriage, religious community, diocese and family is unique. Each person who lives life within these realities is also a unique image of God. And so I will offer more particular experiences for reflection, in the hope that the similarities and the differences of living out human sexuality will both affirm and challenge your own sexual experience, understanding, values and actions.

It is also tempting to focus on, defend or question the rules and guidelines that Catholicism is so well known for in the realm of sexuality. I have a great respect for those ethical rules and guidelines; they aim to protect the value of human dignity, the gift of life, and our relationships with God and each other. We all need to learn about and seek to integrate the wisdom that comes to us in the stories and experiences of those who have given us faith and its ethical convictions. Living our sexuality, however, is not primarily an encounter with rules. Living sexuality is a journey in loving people like God loves them, even when we are tempted to cover ourselves, to hide, to justify our selfishness, or to point fingers. So I will also resist the temptation to focus on rules and turn instead to the real-life moments where we face and live with our sexuality.

Cameron is three and has become very interested in the difference between boys and girls since the arrival of his baby sister. In the bathtub, he keeps asking to name all the parts of the body. He likes to run around without clothes on after the bath, and his parents let him do that when they are home alone. But they have recently introduced the idea of privacy to Cameron. When they have company, he has to get his pyjamas on before he can leave the bathroom. He's not impressed with the idea, but he has noticed that the guests are wearing clothes.

Bryn is turning nine next week. Her best friend, Ethan, lives next door. She's planning the all-important birthday party with her mom. All the birthday parties she has been to this year have been all-girl parties with very girly activities, and one of her friends at school has been teasing her about Ethan being her boyfriend. Bryn doesn't want to be teased but she also doesn't want to have a birthday party without Ethan. To affirm all of Bryn's relationships and her maturity, her mom suggests they have cake and ice cream at the zoo and invite boys and girls and their families to come. Bryn thinks that is a great idea.

Kayla is thirteen. She's noticed lately that she and her friends talk about boys most of the time. Kayla's friends are curious about sex, and so is she, but she doesn't feel very comfortable talking about it with anyone. Occasionally, she talks about sex with her brother, Peter. Peter has a girlfriend who he has not slept with but he says that his body never lets him stop thinking about it. He's not having sex because one of his friends got a girl pregnant last year and he doesn't want to go there. Kayla isn't sure yet that she ever wants to have sex. It sounds like it would hurt.

Ericka was four when her uncle started "playing house" with her. She was seven when her mom found out and made sure that it ended. Though she has had help in dealing with the abuse, she has struggled with how to interact with boys and men ever since. During her teenage years, she did not know how to dress and found compliments about her appearance extremely confusing. At twenty-one, she is contemplating joining an order of religious women so she doesn't have to interact with men. The sister who meets with potential members has just figured out that Ericka is trying to use celibacy and the order as an escape, and both she and Ericka agree that you don't choose a vocation based on fear. It's going to be a long year.

Fr. Matthew has been a priest for five years. Before he entered the seminary, he had been engaged to a wonderful woman. They ended up realizing that they were in love with the idea of being in love, rather than really in love with each other. After some time, Matthew realized that he wanted it all. He wanted to be a priest and have a wife and family to love. As a Catholic, he had to make a choice. Most of the time, he finds priesthood extremely fulfilling. He enjoys visiting the sick and meeting with young families preparing for baptism. The days go by fast and are full of interesting, faith-filled people. The hard moments are balanced with blessings. But at the end of particularly challenging days, he goes home alone and feels the desire that began in his teenage years. All the basketball, great friendships and distractions in the world don't take the edge off the raw desire. And the edges are harder now because as his friends have started having families, that longing is paired with the ache for a partner to love and children to hold. He knows that he is being fruitful in other ways, that his celibacy allows him many more relationships than his married friends, but he aches just the same.

Quin and Payton have been trying to conceive a baby for five years. Their whole lives seem to revolve around sex. They are eating a special diet, doing tests all the time, trying to avoid situating blame. They have chosen to follow the church's teaching and avoid in vitro fertilization, when many of their friends are pursuing this option. Quin is growing ever more resentful of a church that affirmed his desire to receive children as a blessing from God and at the same time won't let him use a technology that might realize that desire and blessing. Payton is adamant that she doesn't want to use in vitro and now they are fighting about that, too. Worst of all, in the middle of the argument, Payton looks at the calendar and says she's ovulating and they need to make love. They both feel isolated and misunderstood. Sex is just one more thing they have to do tonight.

When her friends were falling in love and getting married, Rose experienced the love of Jesus and responded by becoming a religious sister. For the first twenty-five years of religious life she was graced, in spite of her struggles, with a trust that God offered her the companionship that others lived in marriage. And then she fell in love with a man who sang in the choir she directed. She tried to avoid him, but she couldn't. She became confused with God for allowing it to happen, but several weeks later, she realized that she was seeing the man through God's eyes and didn't need to be afraid. The two of them worked hard to develop a deep friendship. In the process, she discovered a freedom in allowing herself to feel and appreciate sexual desire without demonizing it or rejecting her vows. Today, at seventy-four, she met her old friend for lunch. They talked and laughed and went their separate ways. As Sr. Rose walked home, she thanked God for the gift of desire, much more rare in her experience these days, and for the way it makes her feel so alive.

Colleen and Murray both had their share of teenage sexual encounters before they met. They moved in together after several weeks of dating and found out they were pregnant several months later. Looking back on the experience after twenty years of marriage, they both say they wish they had done things differently. They brought a lot of baggage into their relationship. Colleen had been raped and thought that she had to offer sex to make boys like and respect her so they wouldn't take sex from her. Murray was part of a sports team where girls threw themselves at the players and the guys earned popularity by sleeping around. When their relationship got serious, they both had to correct a lot of misunderstandings about themselves and sex. They had to stop using sex against each other, holding out for revenge and operating as though sex was the only way to show intimacy. It took almost ten years before they both felt like sex was helping them to be better people instead of being a power struggle that generated resentment. They discovered that sex could be an act of forgiveness, of playfulness, of relaxation. They discovered that it was an important part of their marriage, but it was never intended to be the most important part. And now that they are parenting their teenagers, they have been doing a lot of reading and talking with other parents about how to help their kids avoid making the same mistakes they made.

Isla never planned on being thirty-five and single. She enjoys her job, spends lots of time with family and friends and is a board member for two community agencies. She stopped "waiting around" a long time ago and decided to just live her life and let it happen, but that doesn't mean it isn't hard. Going to weddings is always messy – she sometimes brings a date, which leads to unwelcome questions and awkward pressure, and sometimes she doesn't, which leads to more awkward questions and people offering to set her up with their brothers, sons and nephews. Most of the time, she enjoys her life, but there are moments when she still feels like she's missing something. She has a rough day, calls a friend, talks it through, but sometimes she just wants a hug. When her friends are having kids, she worries that she won't ever get to be a mom. Lately, she's been thinking about adopting on her own, but single parenting is hard and it will be controversial and awkward, too.

Yvette and Pavel had three children when they became convinced that they should not be using artificial contraception. Their youngest was ten and Yvette was nearing menopause. They hardly had time for sex anyway and for two years, they continued life and love and making love with a new sense of God's presence in their lives – until they found out Yvette was pregnant. She was forty-eight and they were both terrified. They felt abandoned by God, rather than blessed, when they got the news. It took months for them to let go of their anxiety, which was heightened by complications that threatened Yvette's and the baby's lives during pregnancy. In the seven years that followed the baby's birth until the end of menopause, Yvette and Pavel did not make love even once, out of fear. They continued to discern that God was calling them not to use artificial contraception and they felt called not to have any more babies. Many nights they held each other and cried themselves to sleep, feeling deeply the isolation of their married solitude.

Emily and Fred moved into a seniors' home last year when the physical demands of caring for each other became overwhelming. Their sexuality has gone through its seasons of intensity and frustration, presence and absence. Sex has been a gift to their marriage, challenging them to listen more deeply to each other, to be more caring, to share household responsibilities more fairly and to be generous both inside and outside the bedroom. But the hardest thing about the seniors' home is that they cannot share a bed or even a room. For sixty-seven years, Emily has waited to feel the squeeze of Fred's hand before she drifts off to sleep. Fred has been comforted from his nightmares by just looking for his wife's sleeping face. And how they long to reach for each other in the night.

Shawn was fifty-four when breast cancer took his wife's life. He was thankful he got the chance to say goodbye to Rita, to talk with her about their life together and about the rest of his life. In the two years since her death, Shawn still feels like he's grieving most of the time. His counsellor says there is no "normal" grieving time, so he keeps taking it one day at a time. Being married to Rita pushed Shawn out into the world. When she encouraged him, he felt like he could do anything. Her trust and faith in him fuelled him to work hard and to enjoy the fruits of his labour. She had always been awestruck by their kids, and her awe reminded him to take the time to discover each of them over and over again. Some of his colleagues have been gently suggesting that he go out on a few dates. But he knows he's not ready, and he's not sure he ever will be. When he's most tired of being tired, he just wants to rest his head on the curve of Rita's hip and hear *her* voice. He wants to give himself to his wife. To be safe giving himself to her, to the woman who spilled coffee on his pants on their first date, carried their children, got annoyed when he left his coat on the railing.

As a young woman called to marriage, motherhood and ministry, I am constantly challenged by the image of sex as the free, full and fruitful giving of self between spouses. At a theological level, I understand, appreciate and agree with the call from God to offer whole self, without reservation, without coercion, to an intimate encounter that offers the potential of new life (in the form of a baby, but also in the life of the married couple, through forgiveness, generosity, laughter and relaxation). My experience of sex in marriage, however, is that it is at its best a celebration of whatever we have left. At the end of the day, we arrive in the bedroom carrying the baggage of two weeks of interrupted sleep, one sore throat, four loads of laundry, six frustrating days at one job and a promotion at the other, a fabulous but exhausting weekend with the in-laws, and another argument over the recycling. I am worried about a difficult conversation I had at work that day. He is thinking about the mountain of paperwork that awaits him tomorrow. The sex is nothing like the romance and perfection of the movies, nor like the imagined piety of a well-planned act of worship. But it is the two of us, faithfully offering whatever we have left, freely choosing to let go of the reasons to just fall asleep. We bring the fullness of our imperfection with a dose of humour. And we accept whatever gifts and grace, expected or otherwise, flow from showing up to play. Theology and life come together when we can recognize that whatever we have is enough to offer, to God and to each other.

We channel sexual creativity by taking up creative hobbies, making art and music, writing poetry and journals, going to art galleries and concerts. We learn to dance. We enjoy the experiences of the body, the feeling of a warm shower, the comfort of a hug, the taste of our favourite foods. We play well, train for and run marathons, give our creativity over to the projects and people we work with. We feel something of sexual release when we get lost in the beauty of a still lake in the morning, are captivated by the beauty of a piece of music, or enjoy sitting in peaceful silence with a good friend. Just as we reach out to tighten our grasp on the moment, it is gone: an elusive glimpse of something that can only be lived, not possessed. Sexuality, like spirituality, is felt in a deep restlessness, and we satisfy it only temporarily on this side of heaven, whether we are married or not.

Song of Songs reminds us that love is a powerful force and its desire is a flame. Fire keeps us warm, invites us in, helps to feed and nourish us. But it can also burn and destroy us. God's presence in and through our sexuality is not a promise that living it faithfully is easy. At different times in our lives, we will seek healing for our brokenness, find new ways to express our sexual desire, or find that our experience of our sexuality has changed. Sexuality is one more way that we live out self-giving, with discernment and care that will allow our action to be a blessing to us and to each other.

QUESTIONS FOR REFLECTION

1. Whether you are married or single, in a season of joy or difficulty, how do you deal with the longing of sexuality? How do you experience God in times of longing or intense desire?

2. To whom are you called to offer yourself most often? How does your self-giving and receiving of others in those primary relationships prepare you to give yourself to people beyond your family, parishioners or religious community?

3. How has the teaching and wisdom of the church contributed to understanding your sexuality? If who we are and who we become is shaped by how we live, then how has your sexuality affected who you are?

CHAPTER 14

Whatever You Do
to the Least of My Brothers
and Sisters...

"I came that they might have life, and have it abundantly."
~ John 10:10

This whole book is about how our faith is tied up in the body, in the way we live our lives in every moment of every day. In a parable about a king and his people, Jesus tells us that whatever we do to the least of his people, we do to him. When we are impatient with a sibling, room-mate or spouse, we extend that impatience to God. When we ignore the request of a colleague, we ignore the request of God. This is part of the sacramentality of our bodies and Jesus' body. Each of us is a sacrament, according to *Theology of the Body,* making a small measure of the divine visible to the world.

Many of Pope John Paul's writings on justice are rooted in the dignity and sacramentality of the human body. In addressing how we should treat the poor, rely on human labour, share the world's resources and support families (among many other issues), John Paul begins with recognizing ourselves in the other – the experience of original unity. It is one thing for us to talk about "the poor." It is another thing to recognize that we are the poor, that there is no "us" and "them." When we talk about the people affected by violence and strategies for war, we can do so with authenticity only when it is our lives, children and future that are at risk. When we imagine policies that enable women and their partners to carry unexpected pregnancies to birth and beyond, we have to start talking about our families, our daughters and sons. I am not saying that only those people who have experienced poverty, violence and unplanned pregnancy can talk about those issues. I am suggesting that if we take *Theology of the Body* seriously, then we have to shift our mindset away from issues and start to see, hear and love the people who are affected by them, just as we do when we are the ones facing hunger, fear or oppression.

Justice is an action, a virtue we practise that flows from the dehumanizing experience of injustice, from the right understanding that injustice violates God's plan for us, from valuing God's justice. An experience is often at the heart of our work for justice. Jonas is engaged with a homeless shelter because he was homeless in his youth. Renée is passionate about rescuing girls from human trafficking ever since she met a girl in a coffee shop who pleaded for her help. Travis and Jenna give money to a literacy program for refugees because so many of the people they work with have come from other countries and have benefited from the program. The work of justice flows from relationships, from a fundamental recognition that we are created to be our brothers' and sisters' keepers.[9]

When I first read *Theology of the Body*, it was an important part of changing my mind on the church's teaching on family planning. John Paul argues that natural family planning is a discipline, an ascetic action that can draw us into participating in what God is doing in and through us. The idea that natural family planning is like going to bed on time, eating well and exercising made good sense to me. But John Paul doesn't address the justice components of family planning in *Theology of the Body* that flow from his logic. I began with his anthropology, his recognition of the gift of life, of fertility, of sex, and of the discipline of discipleship. The next logical step for me was to extend those gifts to the communities and structures that inform reproductive attitudes and actions. Everyone in the world does not have access to pharmaceuticals and other family planning products. Even if everyone did have access, I am not convinced that it is ethical to think about human fertility in a way that requires massive product consumption. On another note, hormonal contraception is affecting the environment, both in terms of the

9   This is another reference to the *beginning*. Check out Genesis 4:1-16.

packaging, energy and materials required to produce it and in the way that the hormones are released back into lakes and rivers via sewage. People, plants and animals are affected by the estrogen and progesterone that are seeping into the environment. My husband and I choose to use natural family planning because we believe that the church's teaching is right, and because we believe that it is consistent with the teaching on justice as well – because what we do in our family affects the people with whom we share the planet. When natural family planning is difficult and requires sacrifice, the human faces of justice and solidarity keep us faithful when disembodied intellectual conviction might not be enough.

When Rosa lost her job and her pension due to company downsizing during a recession, the company chose profits over people. At a personal level, Rosa looked for other work, wrote letters to the company and the government, and changed her attitude about unemployed people being "lazy." The experience made her work for justice at a personal level. The problem, however, is also political and systemic. The company she worked for is facing rising costs; one of the ways they are "downsizing" is by relocating jobs to markets where working conditions are poor and wages are low. Rosa is starting to see that the ever-increasing demand for more stuff at cheaper prices is driving decision making in companies like the one she worked for. In order to make a difference, many people have to share and empathize with Rosa's experience. They all need to write letters, think about what they purchase and how much they pay, and contribute to changing the political will to provide meaningful work for people at just wages. The solution is neither entirely personal (such as simply getting another job) nor entirely systemic (where we give up on personal solutions because the problems are too big). We have to work at all levels to realize justice, and we have to work together.

When a famine hits in Africa, we can send relief in the form of food from other parts of the world, and we ought to, but this approach doesn't address the problem that national borders have been drawn across God's land, preventing neighbours on one side of the border from sharing with neighbours on the other side. We have to feed hungry people even while we break down the barriers that keep us from sharing the abundance of what God has provided for God's people.

Devon joined the military as a way to pay for school, and he found the people hope-filled and inspiring. He served two tours in Afghanistan. Now that he is home, he knows he participated in some good work. He walked children to school safely, assisted a mother giving birth on the roadside, and taught soldiers how to protect civilians. But he also knows that the military presence has reinforced the idea that weapons are required for safety. His faith tells him that violence is not a way to solve problems; he is working with the military because he sees it making a difference in the world. Devon's dad, who is a pacifist, was disappointed when his son joined the military. His dad supports peace and humanitarian aid organizations that send people into war zones without weapons and bureaucratic declarations. Christmas dinner discussion is passionate and filled with diverse opinions.

Rachel is the director of a crisis pregnancy centre. The organization is small, and although the staff counsel a hundred women annually, they average about twelve births a year. Lots of people support the centre with donations of diapers, formula, clothes and baby supplies. But this year, Rachel is working on a Life is Long campaign. Most of the moms who choose to carry their babies to term lose community support shortly after the baby is born. They don't have access to affordable, quality childcare. They hardly have the money to feed themselves and their babies, let alone cover school supplies, pay for swimming lessons or put some money away in case they lose their minimum wage job next week.

Injustice is rarely simple. Most of the time, it is messy and people are trapped by circumstances that are bigger than they are. When we really see the people who are affected by injustice, when we love those people and we are those people, we hear God calling us to make a difference. We do it in various ways, as the circumstances of our lives allow, and we do it together, as the Body of Christ, because it cannot be done alone.

It makes sense to me that John Paul applies his ideas about our humanity to sexuality first, because we live our sexuality inside our own skin, every day of our lives. We encounter our sexuality at a deeply personal and subjective level – which is part of why we resist any interference or attempt to universalize it. But if we don't explore the objective and universal elements of human sexuality, we risk being duped by the error that our sex is just about us and has nothing to do with justice. On the contrary, it seems to me that if we live our sexuality well, our deep and passionate love for God and God's people has to spill out of the bedroom and into our neighbourhoods, our country and the world. If my love extends only to my spouse and my children, my community members, or people who look like me and think about the world the way I do, then I have drastically misunderstood the experience of original unity. Whatever we do to the least of our brothers and sisters, we do to Jesus. And if we believe in the golden rule (and we do), then the food we share with the hungry is the practical gauge of the food we hope others will offer us when we are in need.

We can spend a lot of time in the church arguing about whether to minister to people's bodies or their souls, or whether my issue is more important than your issue, but the answer is yes. To be human is to be body and soul. To minister to people, we have to say yes to caring for bodies and souls, to protecting embryonic people and the water we all need to sustain daily life. And together, we need to do these things in a way that reverences humanity, creation and God along the way, because it's all a gift and when we stand before God, we want to offer ourselves and the world back to God with an appreciation of its beauty and dignity.

No single one of us can do everything that needs to be done to realize God's justice in the world. But we can learn to see injustice in the world and love the people who are affected by it. We can pick an issue or two and learn a little more about it and what we can do to help. If you aren't sure where to start, John Paul's writings on social justice offer countless options, including the development of just labour laws, hospice care for people dying from AIDS, ethical development and use of science and technology, and caring for the earth so that all people can be blessed by the gifts of creation.

John Paul's numerous and broad applications of the spousal meaning of the body over the course of his pontificate stress just how important it is for us to situate his teaching on sexuality and family planning in his broad call for justice, peace and stability in the family and the world. He challenges us to participate in building a world where each and every one of God's people has the opportunity to live life abundantly. The world is not a simple place, and the decisions and actions that lead us to abundant life require personal sacrifice – a commitment to living our solidarity with a constant awareness of our unity and solidarity with every person on earth. Abundant life is delicate and vulnerable, and it requires us to be attentive to the ways in which the experience of shame tempts us to selfish blindness. The task is large and intimidating, but it is God's work, and God desires to share that work with us. God came that we might have abundant life, and that we might know its cost by our working towards it with him.

QUESTIONS FOR REFLECTION

1. How do you understand justice? How is it related to mercy? How do you see God's justice at work in the world? Where is it absent?

2. How have you experienced injustice in your life? Who experienced it with you? How did you feel? What did you do? Where was God in your experience of injustice?

3. What do you do in your life to be an agent of God's justice? Who are the people at the heart of your passion for justice?

CHAPTER 15

The Harvest is Plentiful

"Go therefore and make disciples of all nations."
~ Matthew 28:19

Because I grew up on a farm, I remember the anticipation of harvest. We watched the fields turn from green to yellow and gold. Our social life revolved, to a certain extent, on whether we were in the fields. We hoped for weeks of hot, sunny weather. We planned meals around the work, eating in the fields or packing lunches to be eaten in the combine and trucks. We counted down the hours and the days until the crop was off. And the whole family lived the harvest.

When Jesus says that "the harvest is plentiful, but the labourers are few" (Matthew 9:37), he is anticipating the harvest. Just as farm families live on the fruit of the harvest, our God longs for his people to be brought in to him. Sharing our faith is a scary thing in a world where people are distancing themselves from religion (at best) or are hostile towards it. But if the God story is our story, then there is no way for us to be disciples who do not share the story.

The invitation to make disciples of all nations is certainly about sharing the God story with people, with the way we live and tell the story of our lives, inviting others to do the same. This invitation, however, is also about our relationships with people. It is our calling to love them at every point on the journey, not only if or when they experience conversion. Love demands that we enter into relationships of love, anticipating resurrection but never trying to force it. In a world where people crave experience, are eager to learn for themselves, to make their own understanding, to live their values with integrity, even if they have to stand alone, "the harvest is plentiful" (Matthew 9:37). Many people are open to things spiritual, and they are finding divinity in creation, in relationships, in meaningful work, in beauty. John Paul's movement from experience to action has been very helpful for me as I think about how I offer myself and receive others in relationships.

The spousal meaning of the body presumes we will be people who give *and* people who receive. When we enter into relationships, we do so because God loves us and everyone else *first*. Our only agenda is love. And we don't just bring love, we receive it. We are drawn into the mystery and wonder of the other person, both of us affected by the encounter. Evangelization that is worthy of the name is a relational exchange of the gifts of God among us. When we share our experience in a way that honours the spousal and redemptive meaning of the body, we must also receive the experience and understanding of others. Our reaching out to share our faith is also an invitation to discover God's presence in the experience of others, to be called to a deeper understanding of God, to more fully value God's values and to act with love.

When John Paul says that our experiences matter, he offers us a way to share the faith that we have lived in the body in a way that is respectful and inviting to others. We do not have to begin with catechesis, with arguments about teaching, with debates over ethical action. We can begin by sharing our experiences and hearing the experiences of others. We can build shared understanding and talk about values. We can be ourselves and welcome others to do the same. Effective evangelization is not forceful, rude, pushy, preachy or judgmental. It is warm and human, inviting and rooted in a desire to love people like God loves them. It is, after all, God's work.

Riley was born into a Catholic family. They went to church, came home, prayed at meals and lived life. Faith was just something he did, not something he thought a lot about. In high school, he avoided the "religious" kids with some intention, but mostly out of confusion. When he left home, he was working with a guy who went to Mass every weekend and seemed pretty "normal." One Sunday, Marco invited him to come to church and then meet up with some friends afterwards for brunch. Riley went because it seemed harmless enough. The conversation at brunch was fascinating for him. For years, Riley had assumed that "normal" young people didn't go to church. But this group of friends talked as easily about the hockey game, their last camping trip, and pop culture as they did about faith. Just as they were leaving the restaurant, one of the girls asked Marco if he was still thinking about becoming a priest. Riley kept his shock to himself, but as soon as they got in the car, Riley asked Marco why he was thinking about priesthood. That conversation is the reason that Riley has raised his family with faith. And that conversation is the reason that Marco has been a priest for seventeen years.

Marla had a really awful experience with church as a child. She was ostracized and bullied by a group of girls her age in the church and she wrote off religion as soon as she escaped their tormenting. Recently, she has had some good conversations about conviction and ritual with one of her cousins. Marla respects Carson. He's smart and he listens well, and he doesn't talk about God to try to bully her into believing what he believes. She is intrigued by his understanding of God and by the way he practises his faith. She feels safe when she is with him, and that sense of safety is slowly changing her understanding of her childhood experience.

For years, Veronika and Trent have made their home a second home to the university students they teach. Veronika went through the Rite of Christian Initiation of Adults several years after marrying Trent and was received into the Roman Catholic Church. For their students, they are a wonderful example of how scholarship and faith can come together in real people. At Christmas and Easter, they host students who cannot travel home alongside their own children and extended families. The dinnertime conversation moves easily from middle school current events to political debate to religious storytelling. No subjects are off limits, and no propositions go unquestioned. Resolution is not expected by the end of the evening, but reading gets recommended, games get played, and invitations are offered for future gatherings, even an invitation to join the family for Mass on Sunday.

Sr. Annette remembers a time when the habit she wore drew people towards her everywhere she went. In the last twenty years, that has changed. People of faith will draw on her wisdom and experience, but the rest of the world is skeptical of, intimidated by or even confused by the way her life looks from the outside. For about ten years, she felt like her order was fighting a losing battle, trying to keep schools and hospitals open and run by sisters, when the world was no longer able to engage them. Then they shifted their mission and strategy – to help evangelize and equip lay Catholics (who are living and working in the world in plain clothes) so they can share God's story with their friends, families and neighbours.

How we share our stories with people and receive their stories is perhaps more important than the actual stories we share. When we sit with our own stories, we discover the way God has touched us over time. We can trace the moments where we held back a bit, needed some space, got interested, rested, rushed in, dove deep, and surfaced. When we look back, we can see where we were pushed too hard or were abandoned. If we can connect deeply with our own needs, we are more likely to approach others with compassion and sensitivity.

Victoria had an abortion when she was seventeen. At the time, she felt trapped. Her dad was very sick and her mom was pouring all her energy into caring for him. She was the eldest of three kids and her mom needed her to take care of the younger two and work part-time to pay for the extra medical bills. She was relieved when her boyfriend suggested the abortion as a way to prevent increasing the pressure on her family. At twenty, she had a nasty run-in with a friend who casually described women who get abortions as "murderers." Victoria's heart went cold. Ten years later, she walks into a park and sees a woman in her sixties standing with a group of people, wearing a sign that reads "I regret my abortion." Tears fill her eyes. She walks a little closer, just close enough to pick up a card off a table at a safe distance away. The woman waves to her and she waves back. She looks at the number on the card and looks up at the woman. The woman nods. Victoria is going to call her tonight.

André has never taken religion seriously. He declared himself an atheist many years ago, and his debates with people of all faiths have always been a form of entertainment, rather than any serious intention to learn. Most of the people he has talked to about religion have been quite content to keep the discussion at the level of being right. And then he met Padma. When he begins with his usual philosophical hesitations about an all-knowing and all-loving God, she doesn't defend her belief of it, she turns the questions back on him: "What kind of God could exist? Does the definition of God prevent God from being?" He's not used to the way she thinks, and her questions are keeping him up at night. She also refuses to let him separate his personal experience from the argument. When he tries to keep it at an intellectual level, she asks him how he feels about his ideas. And then she takes him seriously when other people write him off and walk away. He doesn't know what to do with himself, his ideas or her.

As we go through our lives, seeking God and sharing God's story, we encounter people at particular places in their story – and ours. The gift we offer and receive is who we are together in a single moment. A relationship develops as we share more moments and are transformed by the experiences of one another, our understanding of each other, and the values that emerge in the way we treat each other. We can "de"-vangelize as easily as evangelize, and so we walk with humility, recognizing that no one can be all things to all people, and that we are merely participating in what God has begun and what God will bring to completion – in our own lives and in the lives of others.

My family never used the word "evangelization" when I was growing up, and they certainly do not use it now. Some members of my family practise their faith and others do not. My working for the church does not give me a license to impose myself into their spiritual realities, but it does convey a standing hospitality to talk about faith when they want to, which is more often than some people might think. When people in airplanes or in coffee shops ask me what I do, interesting conversations usually follow. When I am open but not forceful with my life and work, people often feel inclined to talk about spirituality and religion despite the cultural assumption that these subjects are better avoided than addressed.

It is essential that we remember that this mission is God's, and that we are privileged to participate in it, not the other way around. God created the world and everyone in it. God's image is present in each person, and we do not need to "bring Jesus" anywhere. He precedes our effort, our understanding, our longing. Evangelization is not about giving people something they didn't have before, but is about helping them to see what – or who – has been there all along.

Habika has been working for years with women who have experienced abuse at the hands of family members. She uses two principles in her work that keep women referring other women to her. First, she always looks for the right moment to share her own story of escaping an abusive relationship. Her own battle with self-esteem and self-determination puts her on the same level as these women and reminds her that she is privileged to walk with them down some of the hardest roads of their lives. Second, she never assumes she has learned everything there is to know about situations or abuse or God. This principle keeps her asking questions of the women who come to her, digging deeply into how they understand themselves and God. These women teach her new things every day. When she helps out with the Rite of Christian Initiation of Adults in her parish, she insists that every member of the coordinating team work by those same two principles in sharing faith with people interested in joining the church: we must be willing to share our stories if we want others to share theirs with us, and we must always seek to learn something from those who come to learn from us.

A wonderful priest in our diocese spent much of his ministry in a mission in Brazil. When asked why anyone might participate in mission, his eyes lit up in his stiff and wrinkly face. With great effort and joy, he lifted his arms from their resting place in his wheelchair and said, "Go. Go to evangelize and be evangelized!" Making disciples of all nations should make us better disciples, more practised at loving the way God loves.

As part of the Body of Christ, we are called to share in the work and anticipation of the harvest. If we are grateful that others shared faith with us, then we must offer the gift of our faith to others and back to God. We are called to anticipate the joy people find in meeting and getting to know Jesus, just as we anticipate time with friends, favourite holidays and garden-fresh tomatoes. The harvest is plentiful. Making disciples of all nations is as simple as falling in love with God's people, sitting down for coffee with a friend, inviting a new neighbour to dinner.

QUESTIONS FOR REFLECTION

1. Who are the people who shared their God stories with you as you grew in faith? Have you thanked them recently? Who has been blessed by your willingness to share your God story?

2. When have you had a bad experience of someone trying to share faith with you? How did it affect your relationship with God? What allowed you to heal from that experience, to have a new understanding? How did your values shift as a result? And what adjustments have you made to your own action to prevent yourself from hurting others?

3. This week, make a point of telling someone about an experience where the God story became your story. It can be a close friend who shares your faith or someone you don't know well, but who you feel is open to hearing your story. When you are finished telling the story, ask them what they think about the story. How does it feel to tell the story? Did they share a story with you?

CHAPTER 16

Blessed Are They Who...

"Give, and it will be given to you."

~ *Luke 6:38*

In the Gospel of Matthew, Jesus teaches the beatitudes to his disciples. If the God story is our story, then Jesus is still offering these lessons to us now. The words have become so familiar to us that it is easy to forget how radical they are. *Blessed are the poor, the mourning, the meek, the hungry, the merciful, the pure in heart, the peacemakers, and the persecuted.* For most of us, poverty, grief, rejection, hunger, persecution and conflict are experiences we seek to avoid. And yet, no one is entirely successful. The reason that Christianity insists we care for the weak is that eventually, we will discover that we are the weak. We are called to serve the poor so we will open our eyes to see ourselves in them, to realize "they" are actually us. This is a variation on original unity, when we walk down the street and see flesh of our own flesh in the eyes of someone begging for food and money.

The spousal meaning of the body is not a magical idea that makes living discipleship simple or easy. When John Paul suggests that the ultimate meaning of our embodied existence is to give ourselves away, he connects with the countercultural message of the beatitudes. When we recognize that everything is a gift, we are free to give away everything, even ourselves. It is when we are empty that we can be filled. John Paul's *Theology of the Body* invites us to live by pouring ourselves out, even when we feel poverty, grief, fear, persecution, thirst, anger and violence. The self-giving that John Paul is calling us to presumes a healthy and safe environment that respects our dignity. John Paul is not suggesting that holiness is found in allowing ourselves to be victimized or abused. This is a fine line we walk in enduring suffering that has the capacity to refine us and overcoming that which is simply destructive. The beatitudes challenge us to honour God with redemptive suffering and to oppose violence and destruction with a righteous anger and profound hope. Even in the midst of suffering, we are called to pour ourselves out and into God with a generous abandon.

I had been giving presentations on *Theology of the Body* for several years when a phone call from Shauna helped me to see how it could offer people the kind of hope John Paul was talking about when he said that we were always called and never condemned. I could hear the tears in Amy's voice as she told me about her experience of listening to my presentation. She had always believed in the permanence of marriage – and still did, even now – and had hoped from before it began that she would grow old, happily married to her husband. Her marriage fell apart for a number of reasons, some of which she might have been able to change, and others which were entirely beyond her control. Countless times since her divorce she had heard Jesus saying to the Pharisees that divorce had not been part of the plan *in the beginning*. For years, every time she walked into her church, she felt like the woman caught in adultery who was thrown at the feet of Jesus under the threat of stoning. And then she heard the story again, through John Paul's eyes.

Shauna heard about solitude, unity and nakedness, and she associated these with the innocence and hope she experienced in the early days of her marriage. Her shame was not merely the sinful events that led to the collapse of her marriage, but the state in which she had been living ever since. When John Paul follows Jesus back to the beginning, he says that Moses allowed divorce because of hardness of heart, but that "from the beginning it was not so" (Matthew 19:8). As Amy's story was connected to the God story, she felt freed from shame, even as she grew in appreciation that the church doesn't recognize divorce. She had not hoped for divorce, and neither had God. Before marriage, during marriage, and even after marriage, the meaning of her body was still spousal.

With that knowledge, she celebrated the sacrament of Reconciliation at her parish, having realized that she had been condemning herself for all these years. She was created for self-giving, but had been living out of the misunderstanding that divorce had rendered her gift unworthy of being given. She discovered that divorce changed the way she would be offering herself (she would no longer be primarily giving in and through her marriage), but that she was indeed still called to give – to her children, her neighbours, her community and even to her ex-husband, who needed her compassion, empathy and love in a different way.

Amy's story demonstrates just how much our church needs the language and method of John Paul's *Theology of the Body*. The spousal meaning of the body does not apply only to the simple, most comfortable, easy and finished moments of our lives. No one gets married hoping for divorce. We don't go through school looking forward to unemployment or the experience of meaningless and miserable jobs. We don't aspire to be the victims or perpetrators of abuse, violence or trauma. No one shares the announcement of pregnancy anticipating the birth of a child who faces a disability. When we arrive at a place we did not expect to be, we are called back to the *beginning,* to our creation in God's image, to God's desire for us to participate in our redemption so we might share in healing the world. When things don't go as we plan, the spousal meaning of the body remains, and we are called into the moments of our lives with courage and faith that God walks with us there.

Lydia was born with cystic fibrosis. She has struggled to breathe every breath she had ever taken. Her parents thump her little chest twice a day to clear the mucus from her lungs. She is bright and quick-witted, precociously aware of everything going on around her. On her eleventh birthday, she learned that a local charity that granted wishes for children with serious illnesses had provided the money for her family to take a trip to Disneyland. She knows this means that the tests last summer did not go as well as they had all hoped. Lydia can see the fear all over her parents' faces, even though they are trying to hide it from her. Some days she's afraid of dying, but she has been getting very tired these last few months. Every day, she gets up, tries not to cough too much, and sits with her cat, feeling the softness of the fur, the gentle, effortless breaths. She's asking lots of questions, because she's got lots to learn and not many days left to figure out the world. Her parents are making her favourite foods, taking time off work, ensuring that Lydia gets to spend time with her brother and her grandparents. They are all living deeply because there is nothing else to do.

Fr. Ray will celebrate a funeral this afternoon for a teenager who committed suicide – the third in the last year. When he left the seminary more than thirty years ago, he despised funerals and he had thrown up before every one he celebrated for the first year. In time, he had grown to appreciate what he could offer a grieving family, but the celebrations were still hard. Last night, Eileen called. They'd been friends since high school. She asked how he was doing and he couldn't even find words to answer her. "You know," she whispered, "your priesthood has always fit you best when you have held the hands of the grieving." Tears flowed down his face: "I just never stop missing my brother."

Erin and Nick are trying to figure out what is best for Glenn. He has Down's Syndrome and they have cared for him for twenty-eight years. Glenn has taught them (and his sisters) more joy than they could have imagined, and he has depleted their energy. They want him to share in the independence of adulthood, and they feel guilty and saddened when they talk about sending him to a group home. He does not understand the decision, but he is healthy and happy in the day programs he attends. Erin and Nick had many of the same reservations when they sent their girls away to school, watched them marry and start families. This year of trying to decide how to love Glenn has been a Lenten year, a year of sombre waiting, a year of disciplined resistance to the temptation to avoid making a decision. Erin and Nick have lived these Lenten years before and they know an Easter season will come, even if they do not know exactly when. They just keep getting up, eating breakfast with Glenn, helping him wait for the bus. They show up, watch and pray.

Margaret and Joe are politicians in neighbouring ridings, but represent opposing parties. Last week, Margaret took a shot at Joe during question period over his bill on prison reform. It was a personal attack, a dirty attempt to suggest that he has an inappropriate empathy for criminals because his brother is serving time for possessing and distributing child pornography. Joe has been an advocate for prison reform for two decades, long before his brother was arrested and even before his political career began. Joe resisted the temptation to personalize his response in formal debate, but on the weekend, while walking the dog in the park by his house, he sees Margaret walking towards him from the opposite direction. He desperately wants to tell her how upset he is with her, how embarrassed his sister-in-law is feeling this week, how frustrated he is with his brother's refusal to admit he has a problem. He wants to scream at her and threaten to use her family against her. But he doesn't. As she gets closer, he extends his hand to her. She shakes his hand, awkwardly, knowing he didn't have to offer it. They exchange small talk. When she is about to leave, he says, "Margaret, I would really like to tour the provincial penitentiary with you next month. I know we disagree on the principles of reform, but I would like to hear about how you think we should be addressing the problem."

It took Corey three years to get up the courage to tell his family and his church what he had known for a long time. When he came out of the closet, there were mixed reactions, as he knew there would be. I remember sitting in a coffee shop with him one day, talking about faith and life. He was struggling with how to be fully Catholic and fully himself. He was frustrated that his life plays out in two parallel worlds that almost never intersect – with those who accept his sexual orientation and with those who share his faith. He was not in a relationship and wasn't sure if he was looking. He wanted to offer himself in love to the world, but he didn't know how. As I listened to him, tears of compassion fell down my cheeks.

Maya and Luc were high school sweethearts. While they were dating, he was diagnosed with multiple sclerosis. They were the first of their friends to get married, but as their friends celebrated weddings and baptisms, Maya and Luc started to talk about their years of struggle with infertility. Their doctors couldn't figure out why they weren't conceiving, and it didn't seem to be related to Luc's MS. Everything looked fine, but pregnancy never came. About eight years into the marriage, they conceived, only to lose their baby to miscarriage when Maya was just eight weeks along. Despite his disease being well under control, adoption was denied to them. When their siblings and friends have babies, Maya and Luc are almost always among the first visitors, bearing gifts and food for the freezer. It's hard for them to go and see these new babies, and even harder for their friends and family to watch them, but they visit because they choose to be blessed instead of bitter.

When I was going to university, my dad was in a bad accident on the farm. He was checking the cattle on an ATV when he hit a badger hole and was thrown from the vehicle. The four-wheeled machine landed on top of him. When I went to visit him in the hospital a couple of weeks later, he asked me to help him take a shower. It was awkward for him to ask and for me to say yes. We made our way slowly to the shower room. He sat in his wheelchair and I carefully washed his back, stained with bruises, purple, blue and black. I was so grateful to have him sitting there. I washed his hair and rinsed it. I handed him the shower head and he slowly washed where he could. His gratitude was so moving that I could almost see it – gratitude for the simplicity of water, running over his body, for the ability to take a shower. I was overwhelmed by the gift of the moment, washing the hands that had washed me as a child. His injury might have been fatal; he might have asked someone else to assist him; I might not have come to the hospital that day.

When Brad got laid off during a slow season in the mine, he hadn't been too worried. Every year since he had started, some of the staff was laid off in the winter and rehired in the spring. But by May, there was no sign that he would be going back to work. He had never finished the program at the college that he started ten years ago because he didn't like turning down shifts at the mine. But the real reason was that he didn't like school. He did well enough, but he felt like he had to work way too hard to keep up with everyone else. He always felt he wasn't smart enough. And now he feels too old to start again. His wife has no idea how to help him. She sees his embarrassment, and the way that the waiting and the restlessness are eating away at his confidence. She knows he is a good worker, that he can and will find a job he loves, but she wishes she could make him believe it himself. She is working extra shifts to ensure they won't fall behind and is trying to ensure that they spend time with the friends and family who bolster Brad's confidence. Her heart is aching for her husband and her legs are burning from the extended hours, but she's holding her tongue and her husband's hands, for the time being.

Each of these stories is a glimpse of a particular moment in time. While the telling of these stories in short form can make them seem unreal or idealized, none of these situations is easy and most of them were surrounded by no small measure of pain, confusion and suffering.

Theology of the Body does not offer us a way around difficult and unexpected circumstances. A new philosophy or outlook will not eliminate our suffering. Living the spousal meaning of the body means showing up for our lives and facing the moments that lie before us, with a desire to give whatever we have – even if we think it's not much.

Some of the greatest lessons of my life have come from the most unexpected places. Through the bars of a prison cell, I shook the hand of a man who murdered two people. He looked small and scared, like I imagined he must have looked at age six after waking up from a bad dream. He told me about his parents, good people, and how much his mistakes were hurting them. He told me about his battle with bi-polar disorder and how much he wished he could take back that awful night. I also sat with man who sells drugs to anyone who will buy them, who recruits boys to gangs and girls to prostitution rings and has no intention of stopping. I sat with a prison chaplain hours later, crying, moved by how easily their circumstances might have been mine. I was ashamed by their willingness to share with me, while I constantly hide behind the perception that I have got it all together.

When I was struggling with postpartum depression, I sat in a pew at the Good Friday liturgy. Jesus enters the tomb, and the wisdom of our tradition has us go there with him, every year, commemorating his suffering and death. God goes into the darkness and we can do nothing to change his circumstances. But we can go there with him and he with us. I thought of how supportive my family had been during my depression. They could not fix it, change it or take it away. They just surrounded me with care. So many times, I begged God to intervene, to make things go my way, and all of a sudden, on Good Friday, I was moved to tears by the God who simply and respectfully sits with us in darkness as well as light.

The spousal meaning of the body remains even when life includes disability, disappointment, infertility, violence, addiction and death. Our humanity is no less holy ground whether the source of the brokenness in our lives is rooted in sinfulness, genetics, circumstance or bad luck. These stories illustrate that we live out the meaning of our bodies in relationships with other people – people who suffer with us, who share our grace and our brokenness. There is no way around life's difficulties. Just as we offer our gifts, our strengths and our abilities to the world to be blessed, we offer ourselves also in our weakness, our inability and our brokenness.

When things go wrong, I find myself back at the *beginning*. My inability to change the circumstances of the other or to break the boundaries of solitude is overwhelming. At the same time, my heart aches because I recognize that their humanity is also my humanity, and their suffering is also mine. I am challenged to live the vulnerability of nakedness even while I refuse to be held captive by shame.

When Jesus asks us to give, he does not qualify that request. Young and old, healthy and diseased, able-bodied and differently abled, gay and straight, happily married and unfortunately divorced, in our living and in our dying, we are called to give. When it comes to living our faith in the body, St. Paul expresses the coexistence of suffering and hope beautifully: "We are afflicted in every way, but not crushed; perplexed, but not driven to despair, persecuted, but not forsaken, struck down, but not destroyed; always carrying in the body the death of Jesus, so that the life of Jesus may also be made visible in our bodies" (2 Corinthians 4:8-10). Despite the unsettling nature of the idea, it is in our dying that we find the meaning of our living.

To offer ourselves in the midst of our weakness is not to justify or give ourselves over to sinfulness; to continue to give in the midst of it, however, is to share in God's hope for us. Our living is a celebration of God's mercy and God's life. And all around us, even in us, God is pouring himself out to be broken and raised again.

QUESTIONS FOR REFLECTION

1. When has something painful also been beautiful or significant in your life? What were you asked to give? How did that giving feel? How was your body a part of that giving?

2. What weakness, darkness or brokenness exists in you that you find hard to love? How do you live with the blessedness and brokenness inside you? How do you give both to God?

3. What gives you the courage to face the most difficult circumstances in your life? Who do you call on when you do not have the resources to face these situations alone? How is God present to you in those times?

CONCLUSION

A Theology for
the Body of Christ

I was driving home from work one day, turning right at a four-way stop, when I noticed the other cars at the intersection in a whole new way. Instead of simply evaluating which vehicle had stopped first, second and so on, I saw the exchange happening from above, and also saw it extending beyond this intersection. At precisely the same moment that I turned right, the car on the opposite corner did the same. It seemed to reflect something of the beauty of two dancers performing the same action in reverse on two corners of a stage. My errand was part of the dance of humanity, and my life not only has consequence for me and my family, but is part of the ongoing work of creation. I saw, in my mind's eye, a glimpse of the beauty and vastness that is any single moment of God watching us, feeling our urgency, our rest, our joy and our worries. It must be a spectacular sound, the choir of humanity simply singing the song of living. And it is my job to sing my song, to live deeply this life I have been given, because it is here that I am finding a way to be holy, to grow into the salvation that will allow us to live freely with God and each other for all eternity.

When God created the world, he offered us the gift of our existence, to be lived out in the beauty of creation. This is the meaning of our bodies, to offer ourselves back to God in the life we live with each other, walking on the earth. In a letter to the Corinthians, Paul put it this way: "Do you not know that your body is a temple of the Holy Spirit within you, which you have from God, and that you are not your own? For you were bought with a price; therefore glorify God in your body" (1 Corinthians 6:19-20).

When we have an experience of our solitude before God, we have a chance to recognize that our existence is a gift and that we long to share it. Unity challenges us to recognize ourselves in each other. The experience of nakedness calls us forward in vulnerability, to offer whatever we are and whatever we have because we are good. While shame makes this more difficult, Jesus teaches us that the *beginning* matters. God is still calling us to participate in building his kingdom; God has placed his hope in us.

As if this isn't going to take a lifetime to figure out in our own homes, *Theology of the Body* also offers us a challenge as a church: to recognize and love all the parts of our Body, that we may come to appreciate our solitude in and love for the world; to desire and realize unity within the church and beyond it with all of God's people; to open ourselves to the vulnerability and trust of nakedness with one another and for the sake of our credibility in the world; and to do so even while we grapple with our own sin and brokenness.

This church of ours is made up of sinners called to be saints. It is divided both by actual historical splits and by the ongoing division we create by horizontally "excommunicating" the people with whom we would rather not share our version of Christianity. Like the church of every generation before us, we have choices to make. We can give up and stop trying – as many have. We can circle the wagons, tighten control, bully those who disagree with us and attempt to do damage control – it's a tactic we use all too frequently. Or we can choose to place our hope in the God who places his hope in us, with patience, mercy, compassion, justice, faithfulness and love.

As disciples of Jesus, we care for our own broken bodies and the bodies of all of God's people with the knowledge of the resurrection. When we resist the urge to run away from the cross, to disassociate ourselves from the brokenness of the church, we join God in a love that can endure brokenness, division and violence, even while we hope in and work for healing, communion and peace. And when we run away, we will find God in the upper rooms where we hide, calling us back. We will be constantly faced with our own brokenness, even as we are blessed with glimpses of the grace and wholeness brought by the resurrection of Jesus.

We are Christians not only for our own sake, taking up faith simply to ensure our own eternal life. We enter into God's family and get caught up in God's love for the world. The suffering of one child, any child, is our suffering. The joy of one woman, any woman, is our joy. The peace of one man, any man, is our peace. When we can look out at the world, aware that we are in solitude and see unity, we become like God. When we offer ourselves in vulnerability and trust, even in the midst of brokenness, we become like God.

This is the good news of the body: we are called, called with hope, to be the broken Body of Jesus for the sake of the world. So go and live this life that God has given you and us. Live deeply and generously. Fall in love with God's people wherever they are. And live this life so that all of us will be blessed by the gift of your body.